AF531731

HIGHER EDUCATION DYNAMICS

HIGHER EDUCATION DYNAMICS

By

Dr. Nazir Ahamd Gilkar

LL.B., B.Ed., PGDHE

M.Com., M.Phil., Ph.D.

Principal

Sri Pratap College

Srinagar (J&K)

(India)

DISCOVERY PUBLISHING HOUSE PVT. LTD.

NEW DELHI-110 002

Published by:

Tilak Wasan

DISCOVERY PUBLISHING HOUSE PVT. LTD.

4383/4B, Ansari Road, Darya Ganj
New Delhi-110 002 (India)
Phone : +91-11-23279245, 43596064-65
Fax : +91-11-23253475
E-mail : discoverypublishinghouse@gmail.com
sales@discoverypublishinggroup.com
parul.wasan@gmail.com
web : www.discoverypublishinggroup.com

First Edition: **2014**

ISBN: 978-93-5056-469-1

Higher Education Dynamics

Printed at:
Dynamic Printers
Delhi

Preface

The present book, *'Higher Education Dynamics'* primarily is the end-result of occasional papers developed by the author from time to time. A wide range of important themes are covered with a direct impact on higher education system. Higher education now being all inclusive and democratisation of knowledge requires a direct focus towards quality substance enhancement in this era of progress and change. To achieve professional competence, perspective in style the academics ought to be fully equipped with a comprehensive understanding that requires the availability of integrated reading material to them.

The whole text consists of 12 core papers besides 3 seminar presentations also appendixed. A uniform style has been adopted while re-arranging the text material. Every chapter starts with an abstract followed by the conceptual-contextual analysis supported by empirical evidences, exploratory explanations and literature support with reference to the context. To offer an expanded treatment of thought to generate a deep discussion on the topical issues of contemporary relevance has been the preset objective.

The book covers a list of select bibliography at the end of the text to guide the readers in their quest for advanced knowledge in the field. A subject index and a detailed context coverage summary also form part of the book.

I feel highly in-debited and grateful to all those authors and subject matter specialists whose academic works have been consulted and their ideas proven helpful during the course of compiling this work. I am equally thankful to the academics, practitioners and professionals who offered their valued suggestions and comments wherever requested for during the process. I owe an academic debt to Prof. for his kind consent to contribute Foreword. I am grateful to Mr. Muzamil Masood for type writing the manuscript and M/s Discovery Publishing House Pvt. Ltd., New Delhi, for publishing this book well in time in a beautiful style.

Author

Contents

CHAPTER

Higher Education
Enhancing Quality towards Managing Future

ABSTRACT

Higher education promotes knowledge and research to the advantage of humankind. The quality in higher education, over the years, has failed to maintain a pace with its fast quantitative expansion. The present paper, accordingly, peeps into certain Innovative approaches that will be operational toward enhancing quality in higher education sector. Empirical evidences have been gathered in this regard under ten different statements (XI-X10). A schedule administered to a sample of teachers in the disincline of Sciences, Social Sciences and Commerce. Simple statistical techniques have been used for comparative analysis of data, thus, collected. A detailed statement-wise discussion vis-a-vis the results of the empirical investigation form an operational part of this paper. The structural framework of the paper is spread over four segments *viz.*: *(i)* Introduction, *(ii)* The Study (Rationale, Objective, Methodology), *(iii)* Results and Discussions and *(iv)* Conclusions.

Introduction

Quality refers to the standard of performance of the object to which it is applied and thus, is applicable to both the systems and products (Sharma, 2004). Quality in educational context refers to a variety of competencies, in different areas of leaning in life (Sidiqui, 2004). Bloom (1956), while discussing Taxonomy of educational Objectives, has categorised learning outcomes into three domains Cognitive, Affective and Psychomotor. The cognitive behaviour has been classified into two main categories:

1. Lower mental process (knowledge, comprehension, application).
2. Higher mental process (analysis, synthesis, evaluation).

The lower mental processes are usually involved in academic talent. The higher mental processes need a due emphasis in order to foster the fullest development of the unique potentialities of each individual to attain the goals of education (Rather, 2002). Higher education promotes knowledge, innovation and research to the advantage of mankind. Today the system of higher education is confronting with challenges of quality management in the context of globalisation and infotech revolution resulted from the world wide economic integration. Thus, higher education, in the context of globalisation, has to improve its quality of creating learning environment, focusing learned faculty and introducing social relevance of curriculum to compete in line with the international standards. The redefined objective removes the gap between higher education and social development and every individual, thus, will acquire ability to positively contribute towards this direction. Accordingly, quality education refers to transforming the consciousness of a person and enriches the following four capabilities in an efficient, effective and excellent manner (Sharma, 2004):

- To think logically, analytically and critically.
- To acquire occupational and work experience to evoke out an honorable living.
- To realise potential for self development so as to become a better person.

- To cultivate a discriminating capability to appreciate and imbibe the emerging values of contemporary times so as to build a healthy and harmonious society.

The Study

A Rationale

The quality in higher education over the decades has failed to keep a pace with the fast quantitative expansion. The Kothari Commission (1966) had, accordingly, observed,... "the situation in higher education is unsatisfactory and even alarming in some ways that the average standards have been falling". Even after a lapse of about two decades a similar; rather more serious concern was expressed in Government of India document, Challenges of Education: The Policy Perspective (1985) with regard to the quality in higher education. The NPE (1986), as a sequel to these critics, made it categorically clear that quality in higher education was its major concern (Siddiqui, 2004). The higher education system in India now is at cross roads and has to poise for facing competition and challenges from within and outside. Under WTO regime, foreign institutions have been making inroads in India. At this juncture, re-engineering of traditional education system through enhancing its quality with committed assurance is need of the hour (Pathan, 2005). Thus, in the aforesaid backdrop the present paper, perspective in nature, has been attempted.

Objectives

The main objective of the present paper has been to foresee the approaches that will be operational for enhancing the quality in higher education, in the years to come, towards human resource development.

Methodology

The schedule containing ten statements (Xl-X10) has been administered to 100 teachers – sciences 40(38), Social Sciences 40(37) and commerce 20(19). Each statement carried a total score of 10 and the respondents availed of the choice to assess each statement to obtain a more reliable response as against 'yes/no' which results in either 100 or zero score. The response was highly encouraging (94%) as these schedules were returned duly assessed within the stipulated time. The data gathered was tabulated on the master sheet and put to faculty-wise and statement-wise analysis. The total scores (TS), Mean scores (X) were computed and ranks, thus assigned to each statement with a view to ascertain the priorities. To confirm the stability and consistency in the data, thus, gathered Standard Deviation (SD) and Co-efficient of variance (CV) have also been computed. The percentage of the scores obtained vis-a-vis total scores worked out in order to ascertain the extent of acceptance of each statement.

Results and Discussion

The scores obtained (Xl-X10) have been aggregated with a view to assess the overall response and accordingly, classified into 'high', 'medium' and 'low' response categories. The results revealed that 64.89 per cent respondents have highly been interested in the identified approaches; whereas, 26.60 per cent of the respondents have moderately been satisfied and the remaining 8.51 per cent expressed a lower level of interest in the same (Table 1.1). The detailed item-wise analysis and discussion follows as under:

Table 1.1: Index of Responses

Scores	Level of Response	Frequency	Percentage
71 and above	High	61	64.89
66-70	Medium	25	26.60
Upto 65	Low	08	08.51
Total		94	100.00

Personality

The educational planners and practitioners will sit together to restore the credibility of education system at all levels. An educational model, accordingly, will be designed to facilitate the actualisation of total personality of the individual – physical, intellectual, ethical, emotional, aesthetical and spiritual potentialities. The non-scholastic abilities, associated with social interaction, play a major role in the development of personality and, thus, will be evaluated in the system of education. Accordingly, necessary steps will be initiated toward institutional autonomy and teacher empowerment.

The faculty of science has been quite stable and consistent in their opinion as the SD = 0.63 and CV = 8.43 per cent have been the lowest (Table 1.2).

Table 1.2: XI Comparative Analysis

Ts	Faculty	Acceptance		Stability		
		%	Rank	X	SD	CV(%)
28	Sciences	71	R9	7.47	0.63	8.43
300	Social Sciences	75	R2	8.11	1.43	17.63
158	Commerce	79	R10	8.32	1.30	15.63

Curriculum

The focus of the curriculum will be to involve students to think deeply, explore and immolate. The depth in knowledge will be promoted through the improvement in examination system, which in turn will revisit quality of teaching, course designing, transaction methods, study habits of students and parental co-operation. To refresh the knowledge of students, besides classroom teaching, through guest lectures, educational games, project work, study tours, public speaking etc. It will ultimately be reflected in better result performance with higher grades and the consequent decrease in the academic wastage.

The faculty of commerce reflected a stability and consistency with regard in these healthy practices as has been evident from the lowest SD 0.89 and CV = 10.18 per cent (Table 1.3).

Table 1.3: XII Comparative Analysis

Ts	Faculty	Acceptance		Stability		
		%	Rank	X	SD	CV(%)
308	Sciences	77	R5	8.10	1.26	15.55
252	Social Sciences	63	R9	6.81	1.48	21.73
166	Commerce	83	R6	8.74	0.89	10.18

Enrolment

The higher education sector through formal mode will not be open for all and sundry. Due to heavy influx, several problems like student unrest, quality deterioration, inadequate facilities have emerged. Based on entrance tests, the students having aptitude for higher learning will be admitted for the courses at the first degree level. However, more ITIs will be setup to train students in hard skills.

The faculty of social sciences positioned these healthy practices at number one (R1) by scoring 308 points (Table 1.4).

Table 1.4: XIII Comparative Analysis

Ts	Faculty	Acceptance		Stability		
		%	Rank	X	SD	CV(%)
336	Sciences	84	R2	8.84	1.74	19.68
308	Social Sciences	77	R1	8.32	1.49	17.91
158	Commerce	84	R5	8.84	1.50	16.97

Performance

The pay structure of the academic as well as supporting staff will be restructured and, thus, will consist of fixed as will as variable components of compensation. The variable component will purely be performance based. Equally career advancement will also be linked to performance. The 360 performance appraisal for the faculty, administration and supporting staff will effectively be implemented. The life-long rigorous learning by the teachers in their respective areas in particular and worldwide affairs in general will be the main thrust area. Faculty wise academic associations will be formed to deliberate on a variety of contemporary issues confronting different subjects. Thus, 'Perform or Perish' will be the new slogan/buzz word.

The stability and consistency in the scores, thus, obtained has been the lowest in case of the faculty of sciences as reflected by the highest SD = 2.06 and CV = 26.44 per cent (Table 1.5).

Table 1.5: XIII Comparative Analysis

Ts	Faculty	Acceptance		Stability		
		%	Rank	X	SD	CV(%)
296	Sciences	74	R7	7.79	2.06	26.44
264	Social Sciences	66	R6	7.14	1.11	15.54
156	Commerce	78	R9	8.21	1.17	14.25

Fee

The fee structure will also register a hike with a view to upgrade physical capital for the institutions out of the funds, thus, generated internally. The full coverage of the prescribed syllabus in each course of study will be the main focus in order to discourage and avoid selective studies. Regular and rigorous tests will be in operation to keep the students fully engaged in their studies. The focus will equally be on inter-disciplinary approach in order to benefit from each other. The presence of students in the institutions will strictly be regulated in accordance with the University statutes. Further, co-curricular activities will play a significant role in the institutional calendar and competency building of the students.

The mean scores gained 7.4 by these healthy practices have been in the range of 6.4 and 8.2 for the faculties of Social science and Commerce respectiveiy (Table 1.6).

Table 1.6: XV Comparative Analysis

Ts	Faculty	Acceptance		Stability		
		%	Rank	X	SD	CV(%)
320	Sciences	80	R4	8.42	1.18	14.01
256	Social Sciences	64	R8	6.92	1.43	20.66
164	Commerce	82	R7	8.63	1.25	14.49

Involvement

The faculty will actively be involved in teaching, research, extension and governance. The publication of the conceptual as well as empirical research works will be monitored and duly acknowledged for career advancement. The faculty will also be engaged in technology assisted teaching based on a set of educational goals to help students identifying essential knowledge, skills and attitudes. The faculty (staff) councils in the colleges will be humming up with the debates and discussions to help in the resolution of various socio-economic issues of the contemporary relevance. The official positions like Dean, Students Welfare. Dean Admissions/Examinations; Dean, Academic Affairs and Programme Officer for NSS and NCC will be established at each college level.

Interestingly, the faculties of science and commerce reflected the uniform level of stability with SD = 1 for each faculty. However, the data gathered from the faculty of commerce has comparatively been more consistent, CV = 11.72 per cent, as against the faculty of sciences, CV = 12.50 per cent (Table 1.7).

Table 1.7: XVI Comparative Analysis

Ts	Faculty	Acceptance		Stability		
		%	Rank	X	SD	CV(%)
304	Sciences	76	R6	8.00	1.00	12.50
272	Social Sciences	68	R5	7.35	1.08	14.69
162	Commerce	81	R8	8.53	1.00	11.72

Utilisation

The libraries and laboratories will find full utilisation of their available capacities through effective presence of students and teachers. The new approach in curriculum designing will depend on problem based learning. The subjects in degree programmes, thus, will be arranged in a logical sequence so that the basic as well as applied subjects go hand in hand. The continuing interaction between the teachers and students and off the class room sittings will occupy a predominant position in the institutional campuses. Moreover, self finance certificate and diploma courses in line with market demand will be launched to open a window for privatisation for which UGC, NAAC and WTO have vociferously been advocating.

The Faculty of Science, however, accorded these healthy practices, the highest prioritisation by positioning at R1 scoring 340 points (Table 1.8).

Table 1.8: XVII Comparative Analysis

Ts	Faculty	Acceptance		Stability		
		%	Rank	X	SD	CV(%)
340	Sciences	85	R1	8.95	1.28	14.30
280	Social Sciences	70	R4	7.57	1.26	16.64
172	Commerce	86	R3	9.05	1.20	13.26

Intervention

The society will have a direct intervention in the governance of the institutions through the Parents Councils, Alumni Associations, Boards of Senior Citizens, thus, constituted at each institutional level. The institutional functioning will be transparent and open for societal scrutiny and appropriate action by the state. The interaction between the higher education and the society will highly be responsive to the new challenges faced by the society. The rationalisation of staff will be according to the student strength and new reframed course combinations assigned to different colleges based on cost benefit analysis.

The faculties of sciences and social sciences have been in agreement by according the similar prioritisation with R10 (Table 1.9).

Table 1.9: XVIII Comparative Analysis

Ts	Faculty	Acceptance		Stability		
		%	Rank	X	SD	CV(%)
276	Sciences	69	R10	7.26	1.59	21.90
248	Social Sciences	62	R10	6.70	1.33	19.85
176	Commerce	88	R2	9.26	0.92	9.96

Interface

The academic-industry interface will be strengthened and projects besides academic bodies will be sponsored by the industry for finding solutions to its problems. The conceiving of the innovative ideas by the faculty for the benefit of the industry will duly be remunerated. The faculty will actively be engaged in consultancy services. The industry will come forward and earmark funds for creating infrastructure and arranging academic events in the institutions of higher learning. Steps will also be initiated to ensure team work to produce synergy and collaborative effort. The faculty of commerce reflected highest stability and also consistency so far as their opinion with regard to these healthy practices as SD = 0.50 and CV = 5.59 per cent have been the lowest (Table 1.10).

Table 1.10: XIX Comparative Analysis

Ts	Faculty	Acceptance		Stability		
		%	Rank	X	SD	CV(%)
328	Sciences	82	R3	8.63	1.34	15.53
260	Social Sciences	65	R7	7.03	1.27	18.07
170	Commerce	85	R4	8.94	0.50	5.59

Implementation

The implementation of a well designed academic calendar, marked increase in effective teaching days and writing of daily diaries of the academic business transacted will be a reality in the management of academic affairs. The faculty will get an opportunity to be on the boards and will come forward with a, strong will to help in the governance of operations and assist management towards the smooth running of the institutional affairs leading to the attainment of the set goals and perceived mission and vision. The efficiency in the educational system will be affected through self motivation of the teachers, students, supporting staff and college administration. There will be no scope for de-motivating people at any level.

Thus, the faculty of commerce accorded these healthy practices the highest preference by according R1 (Table 1.11).

Table 1.11: XX Comparative Analysis

Ts	Faculty	Acceptance		Stability		
		%	Rank	X	SD	CV(%)
288	Sciences	72	R8	7.58	1.33	17.55
292	Social Sciences	73	R3	7.89	1.35	17.11
180	Commerce	90	R1	9.47	1.10	11.62

The aggregate acceptance (81.20%) has attracted by Xiii in scoring 812 points with R1 though reflected a deep volatility and inconsistency as SD (1.58) and CV (18.22%) has been the highest. Against, this Xviii exhibited the lowest score at 700 with a mean score of 7.74 and comparatively moderate stability as well as consistency in the data obtained. The other items in the portfolio gained their acceptance in the range of 8.67 (max) and 7.74 (min) mean scores (Table 1.12).

Table 1.12: Aggregate Analysis

Ts	Healthy Practices	Acceptance		Stability		
		%	Rank	X	SD	CV (%)
340	XI	74.2	R5	7.96	1.12	14.07
726	XII	72.6	R8	7.88	1.21	15.36
812	XIII	81.2	R1	8.67	1.58	18.22
716	XIV	71.6	R9	7.71	1.45	18.81
740	XV	74.0	R6	7.99	1.29	16.15
738	XVI	73.8	R7	7.96	1.03	12.94
792	XVII	79.2	R2	8.52	1.25	14.67
700	XVIII	70.0	R10	7.74	1.28	16.54
758	XIX	75.8	R4	8.20	1.04	12.68
760	XX	76.0	R3	8.31	1.26	15.16

Conclusions

The faculty in the college sector desires a change to move from the present paradigm paralysis to paradigm shift in the system of education as has been evidenced from the aforesaid analysis. Higher education is required to produce critical ability, sharpen intellect and groom ethical behaviours for human development to effect a social change. In the present stressful environment it is equally essential to add the spiritual counseling for inculcation of social appreciation in our students so that they become healthy human beings and vigilantly relaxed citizens. The educational mission of intellectual, moral and spiritual development of a person with total commitment to humanitarian goals is quite essential for a developing society like ours. Thus, challenges of Human Resource Development are met through higher education.

REFERENCES

Pathan, S. N. (2005), Quality Improvement Programme in Higher Education through NAAC, Intellectual Book Bureau, Bhopal.

Sidiqui, M. A. (2004), "Teacher Development and Quality Education", see Mehraj-ud-Din (Ed.) Higher Education in India: Problems and Prospects, 107-118.

Sharma, S. L. (2004), "Higher Education and Quality Control: Some Reflections", see Higher Education in India: Problems and Prospects, 133-146.

Rather, A. R. (2002), "Towards Multi Talent Teaching Approach", Insight, 1(8): 75-84.

Bloom, B. S. (1956), Taxonomy of Educational Objectives, Handbook I Cognitive Domain, McKay.

CHAPTER

2

Higher Education

Turning Weaknesses into Strengths in the Globalised Era

ABSTRACT

The economic liberalisation paved the way for globalisation of educational services under General Agreement on Trade in Services (GATS) in WTO regime. The new educational environment leads to global competition and innovation is the key to competitiveness and to be competitive focus shifts towards excellence. The intense competition, thus, results in the academic diversification and the development of new educational programmes for new customers as well. Accordingly a programme under the name and style of Bachelor of Business Administration (BBA) has been in operation for last several years in the institutions of higher education affiliated to the University of Kashmir Since the programme is passing through its days of infancy and as such confronts with certain constraints The present status paper attempts a S WOT analysis of the programme and examines the current scenario, curriculum management and areas that warrant improvement in quality so as to make the programme more vibrant. Different courses of study of the programme have also been put to a variety of analysis by employing specific methodology in order to meet the challenges being posed by the global players. In this context it merits a mention that the stakeholders in the system, *viz.*: Teachers, Students, Institutional governors, besides curriculum, process, facilities, etc., are affected by the globalisation of educational services.

Introduction

The idea of innovation is the key to competitiveness and to be competitive focus is on quality enhancement. Thus, to build innovative capacity the partnership of a cluster consisting of industry, academia and research and development is required. The intense competition coupled with ever increasing passion for advancement through new vistas of knowledge which has resulted in the development of more educational avenues. This development is true with regard to business education as well where the outburst of knowledge has further been augmented by the LPG wave that has engulfed the whole world over the last quarter century. The situation besides calling for restructuring of the existing business education curricula at all levels necessitated inclusion of certain new courses so as to make business studies more compatible with the changing business scenario at the national and the global level. Accordingly, a new programme under the name and style of Bachelor of Business Administration (BBA) has been in operation for last several years in the institutions of higher learning elsewhere in the country.

The Study

The three years BBA undergraduate programme an embodiment of the latest trends and techniques in business activities has, of late, been introduced in four colleges in Kashmir, *viz.*:

(i) Islamia College of Science and Commerce, Srinagar.

(ii) Government Degree College, Bemina.

(iii) Government Degree College for Women, Nawakadal.

(iv) Government Degree College, Sopore.

The programme is passing through its days of infancy and confronts with certain constraints. The economic liberalisation paved the way for Globalisation of educational services under General Agreement in Trade in Services (GATS) in WTO regime. The 21st century has created a 'borderless education', with a true international flavour which is neither entirely western in orientation nor 'Asian. The quest for new educational system is a blend of Eastern and Westem models (Hindu, 2005). Thus, a new education environment leads to a global competition. The spin-off will be economic benefits, higher talent quotient on the home turf and hope that the students educated would turn as captains of industry or civil services and also become great ambassadors with a view to take care of national interests. Articulate, committed and passionate about their academic endeavours the students, thrive in the competitive environment around them. This is against the aforesaid backdrop that the present paper has been attempted.

Objectives

The paper pursues to achieve the following specific objectives:

- To study the job scenario in the present global era and attempt a SWOT analysis of the BBA programme.
- To examine various aspects of the curriculum management of the programme.
- To identify the areas that warrant improvement towards quality education so as to make the programme more compact and vibrant in order to fit in the global environment.

Methodology

The present study is based on certain experiences gained by the author over the period and strategies to put into practice keeping in view the business environment in the present global era. The literature available on the subject has also been consulted during the course of this study. Different courses of study have been put to a variety of analysis by employing simple statistical techniques.

Analysis and Discussions

The job scenario in global era entails different activities as given in Box 'A' and based on the same self assessment has been attempted to reassess the strengths to find out the skill sets that are possessed right now. It unveils the weaknesses and the skills that are lacking and need to be developed. It accordingly visualises the opportunities that are available and can be availed of and also the threats to be confronted with. Hence, a SWOT analysis of the programme has been highlighted in Box 'B' Also the vision and Mission of the Programme are given in Box 'C'. The students do not learn simply by being told or lectured upon; and lengthy expositions make them feel bored. Consequently, they bunk classes and undertake unwarranted activities. They finally, resort to mugging up or even attempt to indulge in unfair practices in the examinations. The role of teacher in higher education sector is simply that of a facilitator in the process of teaching-leaning and detailed integrated learning approach is exhibited in Box 'D' and the students need to be motivated in order to participate in the process of learning via the following route:

- Reading independently a particular topic before attending the classes.
- Utilising library facilities available in the institutions.
- Discussing the topics with the fellow students.
- Expressing ideas in the class seminars.

Box 'A': Job Scenario in Global Era
• Consolidation of corporates through mergers and acquisitions. • Business organizations have become knowledge based and highly complex. • Jobs have become intellectual and employees intelligent. • Shift form routine practices to differentiation. • Brain power and not bran power in demand. • Knowledge base of the organization is an asset included in the corporate balance sheet. • Managers got freedom form file pushing and paper shifting. • Information technology takes care of most of the office work.

- Electronic mail communicates information and decisions instantly and substantially at low cost and time.
- Organizations have become flat as organizational layers stand minimized.
- Employees have no definite job descriptions as most of the jobs lost for one or two years.
- Regular acquisition of new skills and their application in an entirely new paradigm.
- Remuneration depends on one's contribution to the organization.
- Paradigm shift in price fixation from cost plus to price minus and elimination of all non-value added activities.

Box 'B': SWOT Analysis

Strengths	Weaknesses
• The admissions are based on Common Entrance Test and comparatively better input is attracted. The in take capacity institution-wise is limited to 40 seats. • The strong faculty with high morale is associated with the programme.	• The programme lacks vertical integration, placement training and project work and sans industry-academic interface. • The programme also lacks in vision and mission to prepare the students in the global era and is confronted with inadequate infrastructure facilities.
Opportunities	**Threats**
• The competitive edge can be enjoyed through focus on skill development in communications, IT and other areas. • The willingness of the select faculty to undergo training and development at IIMs in order to enlarge their expertise.	• The programme at operational level does not appear distinct from other academic programmes in many aspects like teaching pedagogy and evaluation. • The programme is apprehended a failure to compete in the global environment.

Box 'C': Vision and Mission		
Vision		
Develop effective and ethical graduates to meet the desired needs of the dynamic business world and serve the society.		
Mission		
To offer students high quality and Value based Career Orientation.	To facilitate students in understanding, and applying both core and specialised Concepts and Practices.	To provide students stimulating and learning-friendly atmosphere to utilise higher level of their Intellectual Capacity.

Box 'D': An Integrated Learning Approach

- To help students to learn and consolidate their understanding of the subjects through full time classroom instructions.
- To adopt case method as an important tool towards learning approach for class room instruction, discussion and evaluation.
- To prepare text books that are specially designed for independent study.
- To promote independent thinking and reasoning in students and also help them in preparing for the examinations.
- To ensure that all students have access to well equipped labs for practical work.
- To offer project work with a view to equip students with practical application of skills relevant to various business situations.
- To enable students to experience in working environment and combine the concepts learned in class room setting with real life situations in organizations during winter internship programmes.
- To organize seminars/workshops with a view to increase the application orientation of the students and expose them to independent leaning and working.
- To conduct term-wise examinations to finally assess and certify the students knowledge and skills in the prescribed areas of study.

Table 2.1 highlights the analysis of syllabi of a particular course of study, *viz.*: Management Accounting and the following steps accordingly have been initiated:

- The syllabi spread over five units with sub units framed by the Board of Studies in Management in the University in respect of this course of study in the first instance has been split up into a number of class sessions for the full academic year. The analysis of syllabi helped to identify the topics to be taken up for discussion week-wise.
- The students have been advised as under:
  - *(i)* to choose one basic text book for this course of study and stick to it. Other books, if necessary have been used to supplement it.
- To go through the subject matter slowly under each topic at the initial stage, recall the main points and jot them down to assess the home take learning.

Evaluation serves a number of purposes that ultimately contribute to the improvement in:

- Curriculum planning, development and transaction.
- Certification and classification of students.
- Diagnosing strengths and weaknesses of students.

Thus, Continuous Internal Assessment (CIA) and Term End Examinations (TEE) have primarily been effective tools in evaluating teaching-learning process. The CIA is to be made continuous throughout the academic session. The CIA carries 20 marks paper-wise and the students are exposed to the different activities with their respective weightage. At the end of the session, the University conducts the examination which carries 80 marks for 5 questions to be attempted with due regard to the unitisation and unit-wise internal choice.

Table 2.2 exhibits the analysis of comparative result performance for 'Financial Management' attempted in respect of a group of 28 students of BBA-2nd year, in order to ascertain correlation between the two components of CIA and CEE. The Table 2.1 thus reveals as under: (*see table 2.1 on next page and table 2.2 page 21*)

Table 2.1: Transaction – Evaluation Operational Plan

Course Title: Management Accounting

Objective: The course is designed to acquaint students with the tools and techniques of accounting as an aid in decision-making.

Unit/ Week	Learning Objectives	Transaction Methodology	Evaluation Methodology	Overview Mechanism
Introduction Wk-1	• (1) General understanding (2) Syllabus analysis (3) Teaching Plan			
Unit I Wk 2-5	Conceptual under-standing	Lecture/ discussion practical exposure (Industrial Visit)	Alternate sat tests	-Home assignment discussions there on -Doubt session
Unit II Wk 6-11	-Conceptual under-standing -Skill development	-Lecture/ discussion -Accounting game -Numerical analysis	Alternate sat tests	-Student present-ations -Doubt sessions
Unit III Wk 12-18	-Conceptual under-standing -Skill development	-Lecture/ discussion/ debate -Numerical analysis	Alternate sat tests	-Oral quiz -Doubt session
Unit IV Wk 19-24	-Conceptual under-standing -Skill development	-Lecture/ discussion/ group discussion -Numerical analysis	Alternate sat tests	-Role plan -Doubt session
Unit V Wk 25-28	-Conceptual under-standing -Skill development	-Lecture/ discussion (Practical Exposure/ (Industrial Visits) -Numerical analysis	Alternate sat tests	-Seminar -Doubt sessions
End up Revision and Review Wk 29-30	(1) Doubt session (2) Written Analysis (multiple choice) (3) Numerical Analysis (4) Oral Quiz			

- The main score of the marks obtained by the group of students has been 46.68 (out of 80) or 58.35 per cent in the TEE contrary to 14.43 (out of 20) or 72.10 per cent in the CIA. Whereas, in the aggregate 61.11 per cent has been the main score of marks obtained by the group of students under study.
- The co-efficient of variation (cv) reveals that the marks obtained in TEE reflected comparatively consistency (cv = 19.25%) as against that of CIA (cv = 2 1.90%). The standard deviation of marks obtained in TEE 8.52 and that of CIA 3 .16 has been comparatively stable in case of CIA.
- The lowest co-efficient of correlation at 0.09 between marks obtained TEE and CIA reflects that the two variables are operating mostly in an independent fashion.

Table 2.2: Comparative Results Performance

Particulars	(X)	(Y)	(X+Y)
Marks obtained (mean)	46.68	14.43	61.11
Mean score (%)	58.35	72.10	61.11
Range of marks	18-62	8-19	33-79
Standard deviation	8.52	3.16	9.36
Co-efficient of variation (%)	18.25	21.90	15.37
Co-efficient of correlation (C x V5 Y)			.09

Note:

- Maximum marks: (X) = 80, (Y) = 20, (X+Y) = 100
- Minimum Marks = (X) = 32, (Y) = 8, (X+Y) = 40
- X denotes Term End Examination (TEE)
- Y denotes Continuous Internal Assessment (CIA)

Table 2.3 reveals an analysis of a select question paper on 'Management Accounting'. 20 per cent of the questions have been classified under statement based questions that needed text book answers with an elaborative discussions. 40 per cent of the questions have been earmarked for numerical analysis that required solving of the numerical problems. The conceptual type questions that demanded text book answers

Table 2.3: Analysis of Question Papers

(Course No. BBA-303 (Management Accounting) Session Dec. 2004

Analysis of Questions										
Units	Statement Based (Nos)	Answer Required	Numerical Analysis	Answer Required	Conceptual Type		Answer Required	Problem Solving		Answer Required
					Nos	Parts		Nos.	Parts	
I	2	Text book	–	Solving of Numeriical Problems	–			–		
II	X		1		X			1	2	Application oriented
III	X		1		1	2	Text book	X		
IV	X		1		1	2	-do-	X		
V	X		1		X			1	X	Application oriented
Total	2		4		2			2		
%age	20		40		20			20		

constituted 20 per cent of the questions. The problem solving question also constituted 20 per cent of the questions and demanded application oriented responses. Thus, the theoretical content in the question paper accounted for 60 per cent and numerical content for 40 per cent.

Conclusions and Suggestions

The conclusions of the present study have been summed up as under:

The continuous internal assessment, an integral part of the evaluation, highlights such dimensions of the students personality which cannot be judged through external examinations. The philosophy of internal assessment and external examination is quite different. Thus, it is not necessary that there shall be high correlation between marks obtained in continuous internal assessment and those in external examination.

The following suggestions are put-forth towards the quality improvement of BBA programme by turning weaknesses into strengths:

- The focus, today is on student centric rather, teacher centered methodology of teaching. Accordingly, Discussion Sessions are to be conducted under an organized plan, with a view to help the students to develop an understanding of the subject. At the outset, the main core of the topic for discussion (communicated earlier) is to be detailed out. During the course of the class session, the students are engaged in effective discussions, regulated by the concerned teachers and at the end the proceedings are summed up point-wise. The students also take notes as an aid to their learning.
- The questioning attitude is required to be encouraged in students for gaining of knowledge. Students are insisted on the clarity of understanding of thought. They shall remain restless till certain doubts are cleared. Hence, based on the study of each chapter the students form questions. Consequently, studies get a pointedness that help in their understanding of the subject. An effort is also to be made

to know the extent of home take learning by them. Thus, to overcome certain difficulties experienced by the students, Doubt sessions are organized regularly and such sessions prove very helpful not only to those who are highly demanding and, as such, raise queries; but, to all those who participate in these innovative sessions. These sessions are provided a unique experience and exposure to the teachers associated with the programme.

- The curriculum requires to be restructured to ensure the incorporation of placement training and project report in order to add dynamism to the programme.
- The style and practice with regard to design of question papers and evaluation of answer scripts needs to be redefined. The traditional approach being practiced presently especially vis-a-vis the pattern of question papers needs to be done away with, the early the best. The question papers should be so constructed that alongwith the long answer type they accommodate different types of tests like objectives, short answer and very short answer type tests with a prescribed limit of words.
- The admission process to the BBA programme has to be taken up simultaneously with other undergraduate courses as per the academic calendar of the University. The proposed change, *inter alia* is expected to attract a large number of students to seek admission for the programme.
- The academic bodies like Board of Undergraduate studies in Management are required to take steps to frame a panel of examiners for setting the question papers and evaluation of answer scripts based on merit and experience of teachers. The panel should strictly be adhered to by the concerned in the office of the Controller of Examinations. Further, priority should be accorded to the teachers associated with the teaching-learning process of BBA programme so that the objectivity of the overall examination process is maintained and enhanced.

- The BBA programme for all the purposes has to be operated on professional lines and, accordingly, AICTE is needed to initiate effective measures to grant affiliation to the institutions operating this programme.
- The courses of study of the programme require a continuous review, through revision with regard to the course contents, instructional objectives and pedagogic methodologies. Thus, to maintain the relevance of this professional programme in the ever changing business environment.
- The course-wise academic load is desired to be distributed evenly. Here a reference may be made to a course of study titled 'Fundamentals of Accountancy'. The paper is content wise too heavy to be completed within the stipulated teaching period as prescribed by the UGC. This course of study, therefore, needs to be redesigned.
- The annual pattern of the examination is required to be replaced by the semester system. The programme needs a continuous teaching-learning and evaluation process which necessitates rigorous and regular exercise by the students as the academic load both in terms of number of courses of study and content is substantial.
- The course content during its transaction has to be correlated to the day to day life problems to make learning effective. Also possibilities have to be explored for enriching learning of the subject matter through motivation by teachers to prove learning fruitful.
- The teachers associated with the teaching of BBA programme necessarily need to be involved in the process of course planning and development in a workshop before the meetings of the BOUS are organized for the purpose. Of course, it will be in the wider academic interests that the recommendations of the workshop based on collective wisdom are considered by the board.
- The courses of study – Theoretical as well as Numerical – need a particular portion of the syllabi content identified for practical orientations.

- The old saying – iron cuts iron – is a gem of wisdom, aptly relevant and suggests a strategy here. The rival is superior mainly because of intellectual superiority. It is knowledge that has given rival a superiority in every field of life and it is through knowledge alone that rival can be countered. Thus, knowledge is the other side of the power. Total commitment to the mission alone can help to outperform the rival players.
- The programme primarily envisages to enable students to acquire and demonstrate a set of relevant competencies in the areas, *viz* problem solving, decision-making creative analysis, communication and leadership. Strenuous efforts in this regard are to be put in towards realising these objectives.
- The learners need to be encouraged for intellectual stimulations which is required to be accorded priority. Thus, to be innovative and urge to question assumptions explore new ideas and methods and approach old situations with new perspectives.
- The immediate steps have to be initiated for the exchange of faculty and students institutions-wise and also development of a joint course with professional institutions and sister university which must focus on job market flexibility and innovative programmes.

In sum, there is all round deterioration in quality education. Successful innovations do not take place without dynamic, committed and energetic academic leadership at the level of policy-making. Also, foresighted and skillful role players at the operational level with determination can turn threats into opportunities.

CHAPTER

3

Higher Education

Teachers' Role in Triangular Paradigm

ABSTRACT

The present paper makes a humble attempt to study the teachers' role towards quality education in HEIs in a triangular paradigm. Varied expectations of society from teachers, teacher empowerment and its implications, chain accountability and interface among different stakeholders have critically been analysed. Finally, the paper sums up the discussion in a lucid way.

Introduction

- *Adopted from NPE (1986):* "A teacher is the principal means for implementing all educational programmes", and 'No people can rise above its teacher". A teacher is thus put at a pivotal position in the educational system in a more meaningful manner. The issue of quality education presents a new range of challenges and poses conceptual and practical problems which are complex in character. The availability of qualified and motivated teachers who pursue teaching as a career option is a necessary prerequisite for quality assurance and sustenance. It is because of the fact that no system of education can rise above the quality of its teachers.

The Study

Babptosh Dutta Committee in August, 1991 made a very interesting revelation, ".............. conventional college teaching is perhaps the greatest social tragedy". To avert this social tragedy there is an urgent need for value creation for society through HEIs. The society has certain expectations from the teachers. The greatest challenge today for quality education is to strengthen participatory democracy in the HEIs. The purpose of 'teacher empowerment or functional freedom' is to bring an improvement in the educational standards with fulcrum being the teacher. Thus, in the backdrop of the aforesaid statement, the teacher empowerment has gained an added significance under new paradigm where quality education has been the main objective. Finally, the focus has to be on the chain accountability revolving around different stakeholders in educational system including teachers. The teachers' role in the aforesaid backdrop can be studied in a triangular paradigm exhibited below:

Objectives

Accordingly, the present paper makes a modest attempt:

- To assess the expectations of society from teachers.
- To study the functional areas within the framework for teacher empowerment.
- To examine the chain accountability process with a special thrust on 360 degree performance appraisal.

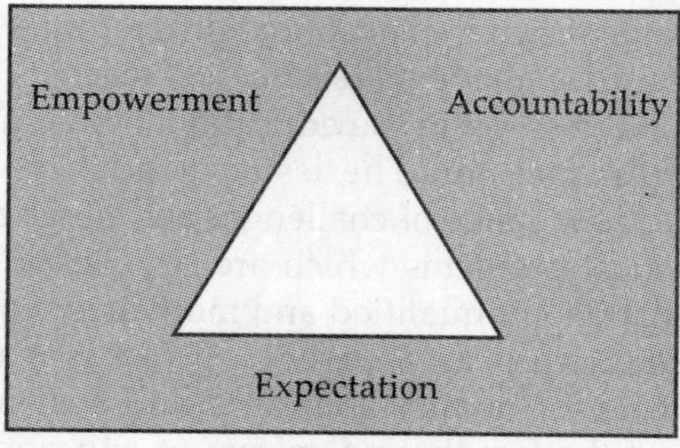

Fig. 3.1:

Contextual Analysis and Discussion

The role of teacher in a triangular paradigm given in Fig. 3.1 is discussed threadbare hereunder:

Expectations

Teachers are said to be 'pillars of the nation'. Sir John Adams calls teacher as if the 'maker of man'. As says Dr. S. Radha Krishnan, "Who can doubt that vedas, the sayings of Buddha, the Holy Qur'an and the Bible embody many of the ideas that have profoundly influenced the development of education. Within each tradition is a concept of the ideal teacher, the priest teacher". Dr. APJ Abdul Kalam says, "A student spends 25000 hrs. in the campus. The school must have the best of teachers who have the ability to teach, love teaching and build moral character". A triangular paradigm based on the societal expectations from teachers given in Fig. 3.2 is further discussed hereunder:

A	Love Teaching	Pursue Mission	Full faith in Profession and Total Commitment
B	Ability to Teach	Develop core competencies	Continue hard work and regular up-graduation
C	Build moral character	Inter-personal relations	Love and affection for those who come to contact with

Tools available to teachers in rendering their professional services

Fig. 3.2

Love Teaching

- To accord academics the highest priority.
- To promote sense of commitment, dedication, and sincerity.
- To make education socially relevant and see the institution serves the social interests.
- To encourage self introspection and accountability.

Teaching Ability

- To continuously upgrade core capabilities.
- To achieve academic excellence.

- To live with dignity in a highly competitive world.
- To cultivate a true academic culture in the institution.

Moral Building

- To promote value based concept of life and make the society a better place to live in; to work for and enable people to explore the truth.
- To forge goodwill and brotherhood and achieve a unique image in the society.
- To encourage students to overcome inhibitions and maintain a true teacher-taught relationship, rather seller-buyer relationship.

Empowerment

- Alvin Toffler 1991 calls this era the 'power shift era' which implies a deep level transformation in the nature of power. Thus.
- Empowerment as a motivational concept is associated with 'enabling rather than 'delegation.
- Empowerment requires the creation of culture which would encourage people at all levels to feel that they can make a difference and also help them to acquire the confidence and skills to do so.
- Empowerment occurs when people are adequately trained, provided with all relevant information; and involved in the decisions.

The implications of Empowerment are given in Table 3.1.

Thus in the resent context teacher empowerment in the HEIs would revolve around the following:

(a) Physical Quality – Curriculum Management.

(b) Interactive Quality – Faculty Development.

(c) Institutional Quality – Corporate Life of the Institution.

Curriculum Management

The workshop on Curriculum Development in each discipline shall precede the BOUS respective meetings, wherein the teachers participate and express their views and share their

Table 3.1: Empowerment Implications

<table>
<tr><th colspan="2">Shift</th><th rowspan="2">Results</th></tr>
<tr><th>From</th><th>To</th></tr>
<tr><td>Suspicion and Fear</td><td>Trust and Challenge</td><td rowspan="7">• People in the organization are valued and encouraged to make personal contributions.
• People are constantly aware as to why and what they are seeking to achieve and how it fits with the organizational goals.
• People work in a culture that is likely to be co-operative, rather than fault-finding one.
• People have a real willingness to take personal responsibility for –
• Their own success.
• Success of the team in which they work.
• Success of the organization as a whole.</td></tr>
<tr><td>Little initiative</td><td>Enthusiasm and Proactive approach</td></tr>
<tr><td>Scant training and development</td><td>Continuous Development</td></tr>
<tr><td>Feedback is seen as a critique</td><td>Feed-back is seen as essential</td></tr>
<tr><td>Lack of Vision</td><td>Strong, focused and shared vision</td></tr>
<tr><td>Problem avoiding attitude</td><td>Problem solving attitude</td></tr>
<tr><td>Close communication</td><td>Open communication
• Sharing of information
• Sharing of ideas
• Sharing of skills</td></tr>
</table>

Source: Constructed on the basis of information obtained from Human Resource Management by Pattnayak B.

experiences and thus learn from each other. This exercise will empower teachers at large to be a part in the course planning and development. The recommendations of these workshops, which provide a wider platform for discussions could be a background material for further deliberations by the BOUS. The teacher empowerment exercise would enable teachers to transact the structured study package primarily designed in these workshops and later on adopted by the BOUS and finally approved by the Academic Council of the affiliating University.

- The teachers must be empowered in the pedagogical methodology and accordingly befitting infrastructure facilities are required to be made available in the classroom setting.
- The existing over – emphasis on annual examinations needs to be minimised and accordingly due reliance has to be placed on the term based examination. The academic session thus is required to be divided into two terms and term-I is to be exclusively managed by the concerned teacher at his/her institutional level with a view to:
    - empower teachers in evaluating their students directly;
    - spread the academic load of students in two terms;
    - relieve students from examination stress and strain;
    - save time consumed in the conduct of examinations.

Faculty Development

Globalisation signifies international competitiveness. Efficiency, effectiveness and competence are raisen d'etre for survival in the global era. Enhancing of the knowledge, skills and professional competence of the faculty is the main focus to accomplish academic objectives and goals in the emerging scenario. Thus.

- Academic Staff Colleges (ASCs) under the UGC scheme in the country are engaged in organizing faculty training and development programmes (Known as Refresher Courses). The ASCs generally have shown tremendous lapses in offering really advanced courses to meet the requirements of the faculty in the changing needs of the country now being merged in the broad spectrum of global economy. An effective co-ordination, therefore, is necessary among the ASCs to discard the old setup and widen their academic canvas having the global recognition.
- The three week Refresher Courses are required to be converted into weekly workshops to save time and every teacher made to attend a week long workshop every year to be abreast with the latest developments made in his/her discipline at global level.

- The faculty in the colleges is being empowered to act as Resource Persons for Education Satellite Network Programme. This will provide an opportunity to every teacher to prepare at least a topic for dissemination through teleconferencing. This will increase the morale of the teachers.
- The PTAC scheme launched by the UGC was a step towards teacher empowerment. The scheme has not been operationalised in the HEIs in our state in letter and spirit and there are many instances where the funds under this scheme were preferred to be lapsed, rather than motivating teachers to present papers at the national level conferences and seminars. Teachers are to be encouraged to attend national level events.
- The faculty has however to make efforts at individual level also for the professional development through continuing education, research and extension and thus work for empowerment at its own as well.
- The faculty is to be enabled to have a minimum functional knowledge of computers in the beginning and gradually the proficiency level will be attained. Time slot in the HEIs needs to be earmarked in the Daily Time Table for the faculty (batch-wise) to have hand on computer operations.

Corporate Life

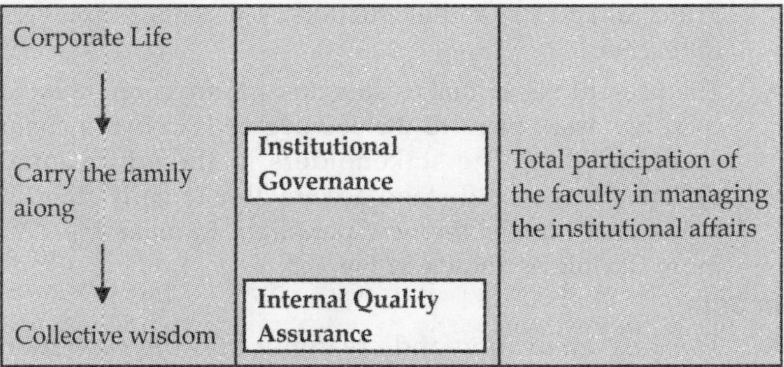

The teachers have a tremendous role in the corporate life of an institution; at least, on account of *(i)* institutional governance scenario that encourages internal quality assurance, sustenance and enhancement. IQACS have been constituted at HEls with a view to ensure overall sustenance find improvement in the quality of education offered by the institutions. The main focus is on the development of a system for conscious and consistent improvement in the performance of these institutions. The faculty has a right to information and can actively involve themselves in decision-making process to contribute positively towards the institutional building and development. Thus a teacher is required to be proactive, rather reactive and always offer his sincere and professional services to make the system operational efficiently and effectively.

Accountability

- The widely debated HRD mechanism that has long term implications in systematically improving the quality standards of education as well as translating the institutional mission and vision into reality is the Performance Appraisal System (PAS).
- The Rastogi committee constituted in August. 1994 recommended a PAS that is transparent, participative and comprehensive. The 360 degree PAS includes teacher self appraisal report together with student evaluation system (bottom-up appraisal), peer evaluation. Evaluation by Principal and up; and evaluation by parents! employers of teacher.
- The present paper makes an extension from one-way to two-way assessment to the 360 degree PAS into a chain accountability. The stakeholders in the educational system. Thus would stand accountable to each other in a link chain under the new paradigm to make the PAS more flexible as shown in Fig. 3.3.

In Sum

- To bring innovation and creativity into the education system and to ensure that the students do not get lost in the structured study packages only.

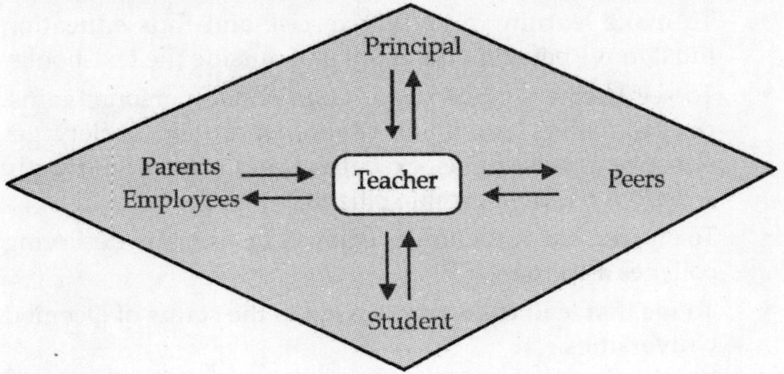

Fig. 3.3: Chain Accountability

- To bring about a change through new skills and new ways of managing education programmes.
- To see that a teacher is fully committed to his job and works hard to re-sharpen his skills regularly by acquiring updated knowledge especially in his discipline.
- To ensure that a teacher maintains good inter-personal relations with his superiors, clientele, colleagues and every one who comes in contact with him.
- To involve teachers in the process of course development by organizing workshop prior to BOUS meetings in each subject.
- To convert three week Refresher Courses into weekly workshops to be attended by the teachers every year with a view to reduce time also keep them conversant with the emerging trends in their respective disciplines.
- To modify the pattern of APRs and the performance evaluation of teachers shall not be swayed by sentimentability but rationality and teachers ranked with due regard to their performance.
- To provide equal opportunity to the teachers to contribute towards Corporate life of an institution.
- To ensure that a teacher contributes his share in academics within the role assigned to him.

- To make learning a joyful exercise and thus education must move beyond classroom and outside the text-books.
- To see teachers place social good above personal gains, people realise true value of education and society get effective professionals, executives and more importantly sensitive and responsible citizens.
- To ensure that autonomy is enjoyed by as many deserving colleges as possible.
- To see that lead colleges are risen to the status of Deemed Universities.
- To ensure quality education and healthy practices through private initiatives encouragement in the educational sector with adequate safeguards.
- To facilitate teachers to be able to draw knowledge from various sources such as internet, digital library, etc.
- To watch teachers remain competent, meet emerging challenges and the needs of the society.
- To bring major examination reforms by adopting continuous internal evaluation and well defined academic auditing.
- To reduce the burden of course load by introduction of semester system at under-graduate level.
- To provide teachers necessary infrastructural support that they need to teach students and maintain quality standards that the 21st Century demands.
- To create an environment for proper initiative and self-motivation in order to render teaching more effective so that the profession becomes more attractive.
- To lay greater emphasis on continuing self-education by teachers to meet the growing demands of teaching profession.
- To facilitate on-line teaching (tele-conferencing methodology) to interact with the students and be able to clarify their doubts as if they are in the same simulated classroom setting.

REFERENCES

Alvin Toffler (1991), "Future Sheeks".

Wley A (l934), The way and the power: A Study of the Tao Te Ching and its Place in Chinese thought, Alleny and Lawlleo E. (1992). The Ultimate Advantage, Jossey-Bass, San Francisco, CA Greenberg J. and Barren R. (1997), Behaviour in Organization, 6th Edition, Prentice-Holen, Upper Saddle River, NJ.

Pattnayak B (2001), Human Resource Management Prentice Hall of India, New Delhi.

Cenger JA and Kanungo RN (1998), The Empowerment Process: Integrating Theory and Practice, *Academy of Management Journal*, 13, 471-482.

CHAPTER

4

Higher Education

Empirical Investigation Highlighting New Education Technology

ABSTRACT

The present paper highlights the significance of new educational technology intervention, instructional transaction and attempts to study the capacity building and utilisation of facilities created, thus, by the Faculty in the College sector in Kashmir. The paper also focuses on the key trends that will take shape in future in this context. (Gilkar, 2006).

Introduction

Top priority among seven point criteria assessment and accreditation by NAAC has been accorded to 'Teaching-learning evaluation' as this criterion carries 2/5" of the total Weightage. Teaching methodology, multi faceted concept, is embodied *inter alia* with technological intervention. Regular and rigorous changes have been adopted towards improvement in instructional strategies as a culture, and accordingly, adequate and appropriate arrangements are made to facilitate the stipulated changes. The educational technology intervention in education has certain objectives, *viz.*: to provide an improved teaching-learning climate in and outside the class room setting, to enhance scope for new instructional strategies, to offer opportunity to supplement, rather than replacement of the conventional instruction transaction.

The Study

Need

The paper focuses on the future key trends with a view to develop a vision anchored around tomorrow's technology aided education, tomorrow's competitive environment and tomorrow's dynamic society. Of course, backward linkages in this regard have also been maintained. With this back-ground the present paper has made an attempt to examine the state of affairs in college sector in Kashmir with reference to certain select technologies.

Objectives

Thus, the present paper pursues certain objectives as given here under:

- To have a conceptual understanding of the new educational technology.
- To gather an empirical evidence with regard to the technological intervention in the institutions of higher learning in Kashmir in respect of capacity building and its utilisation.
- To focus on future perspective keeping in view the requirements of emerging highly competitive environment.

Methodology

The paper is based on the available literature on the subject and survey of various colleges in respect of capacity building and corresponding utilisation of the facilities created.

Discussion

Conceptual Frame Work

The educational technology as a tool is primarily utilised with a view to:

(i) improve teaching-learning process;

(ii) enhance concretisation of concepts;

(iii) classify abstract ideas;

(iv) forge skill transformation etc.

The technology intervention in education helps thus:

(a) teaching machine implements programmed instruction;

(b) internet a resource in and outside the classroom level;

(c) use of electronic mail in the instruction of higher learning because of transformation from teacher-centered to learner centered mechanism; and

(d) tele-conferencing sessions held for guiding learners in remote places, and interactive learning network through tele-conferencing provides environment for face to face conferencing (Pathan 2005).

The knowledge of pedagogy in teaching with technology support can be judged in respect of:

(i) familiarity of faculty with the application of technology supplemented teaching;

(ii) interest shown by the faculty in handling new educational technology;

(iii) capacity of the faculty in generating technology aided content; and

(iv) expertise of the faculty in e-media, multi-media and computer aided packages.

The technological empowerment thus provides opportunities for:

(i) capacity building;

(ii) exposure to mass media;

(iii) appropriate training programme; and

(iv) educational specific technologies.

The communication satellite for educational development focus on:

(i) TV and Radio based development;

(ii) internet based development.

Thus, the third wave of technology has revolutionised education sector through internet based development.

- The internet based education is regarded as one of the most significant and the best way in teaching learning process.

- The advent of web technology has brought radical changes in human outlook; thus revolutionised all walks of life including education sector.
- The use of multimedia in e-content development through Edu-sat has given new face to higher education to raise the quality standards of teaching process to new heights.
- The new technological advancement.

However, on the basis of age, College sector in Kashmir has been classified under categories so far as capacity building is concerned.

- Old generation colleges that have built capacity over the years of their existence.
- Young and comparatively less enriched colleges as regards new technology.
- New born colleges which are still housed in 2-3 hired rooms.

The institution-wise status of capacity building in technology with regard to the old generation colleges is highlighted in Table 4.1.

Table 4.1: Capacity Building

Institution	TV/ VCR	LCD Projector	Over Head Projector	Slide Projector	Modern Equipped Classroom
Government College, Baramulla (B)	5	3	3	2	1
Government College, Bemina	4	3	2	1	–
Government College, Ananatnag (B)	4	–	2	2	1
S. P. College (B)	5	3	3	3	1
A.S. College	5	4	3	3	1
Islamia College	6	7	9	3	1
Gandhi College	–	2	–	–	–
Womens College, MA Road	5	5	7	3	1
Womens College, Nawakadal	2	4	2	1	–
Government College, Sopore	1	3	1	–	1

The study reveals that:

The facilities have not been built up on equal footing in all the colleges falling under the same category.

The facilities created are not commensurate to the student strength. The use of facilities, whatsoever, is very limited and even negligible. Variety of factors have been identified for being responsible for non-utilisation of these facilities:

1. System of education is subordinate to examinations.
2. Examination system itself is defective as the thrust is on rote memorisation only.
3. Working environment is non-competitive. Thus, there is no scope for innovations and differentiation.
4. Lecture method and even note dictations are commonly used.
5. Classrooms are not spacious and equipped with state-of-art facilities.
6. Facilities available, what so ever, are not used for syllabi transaction and so on.

Managing Future

It is however foreseen that in future certain drastic changes will take place. As a sequel to these changes various developments will emerge like:

- *(i)* Higher education (through formal mode) will not be open for all.
- *(ii)* Emphasis will be on learning and understanding of the concepts not cramming of the text.
- *(iii)* Central facilities at institutional level in the shape of a Modern Equipped class room will be created.
- *(vi)* Faculty will be self-motivated and will love the intervention of new technology in syllabi transaction. Syllabi will be analysed and selected topics from each unit will be transacted with the application of new technology;
- *(vi)* Time table will be re-scheduled to create space for utilising central facilities built up.

(vii) Faculty will be exposed to the use of audio-video aids and will make liberal use of the facilities thus created in the institutions.

(viii) Focus will be on performance measurement of faculty with regard to academic contributions and the utilisation of new technology in the transaction of syllabi.

Conclusion

The technology integration with class room curriculum is becoming an inseparable part of effective teaching every passing day and, thus initiatives are desired in this context to meet challenges that force faculty to adopt new developments.

REFERENCES

Pathan, S.N (2005), Quality Improvement Programme in Higher Education through NAAC, Intellectual Book Bureau, Bhopal.

CHAPTER

5

Higher Education

Linkage Modes Regarding Corporate Academic Interface

ABSTRACT

The globalised era demands to establish a strong relationship between industry and academia. Accordingly the present study attempts to identify the various linkage modes through which both these constituents work in close tandem. An empirical survey has been conducted to assess the present status of such an interface in commerce colleges operating in Jammu and Kashmir. At least 10 parameters such as:

1. Corporate journalism.
2. Event management.
3. Industrial governance.
4. Training and development.
5. Curriculum designing.
6. Industrial tour.
7. Research projects.
8. Placement cells.
9. Consultancy services.
10. Corporate exposure have been evaluated.

The study is divided into four parts:

(i) Backdrop highlighting areas of mutual interest.

(ii) The study underlying rationale, objectives and methodology.

(iii) Results of survey and discussions there upon.

(iv) Conclusions.

Introduction

The business has an enormous stake in commerce education and vice versa. The output of commerce institutions is a befitting input for the business enterprises. It is thus imperative for commerce – academics and business managers to sit together and deliberate upon the issues of their mutual interest. The success of the corporate academia interface is based on the following assumptions (Gilkar, 2003) that:

- The commerce academics and business managers possess adequate capabilities that can be exchanged gainfully on the basis of win-win strategy.
- The business managers should make clear the type of commerce graduates they need to satisfy their requirements to make the commerce curriculum effective and result oriented. In workshops of 'Designing Commerce Curriculum' periodically organized, their participation in the deliberations is essential to elicit cross sectional views.
- The commerce academics and the business mangers need join their hands in order to identify the problems to be addressed by the researchers and the Board of Research Studies in Commerce. There must be people present on the boards from the industry as well.
- The students of commerce are encouraged to visit the industrial estates for 'in-plant training' in different functional areas based on their specialisations.
- The commerce academics can offer consultancy services to the industry in the areas like – entrepreneurship development, Financial engineering, cost management, tax planning, etc. Such consultancy services have at least

an advantage for the teachers that they can improve their quality of teaching.

- The commerce teachers may stay for some time in the industrial enterprises preferably during long vacations and work there on some of its problems. They would thus be exposed to the practical implications of the management theories and commercial practices. It would result in teaching the commerce curriculum in more effective and result oriented fashion.
- The business managers can be invited in the colleges as guest speakers. This arrangement would cement an effective linkage between theory and practice.
- The industrial enterprises are benefited by way of educated and trained manpower produced by the educational institutions. The industry needs to earmark adequate funds to support variety of activities conducted like seminars, conferences, and workshops. Arrangements for the Business Education Study Tours (BEST) to be a regular activity conducted by the institutions.
- The faculty is provided a space to develop case studies especially in the local context to be used as instructional pedagogy during curriculum transaction in the regular classroom setting.

The Study

Rationale

The relevance of business education to the current requirements of industry in the country is being highly realised. The industry and academia are mutually interdependent. Sharma and Singh (2007) thus opine that due to advancement of technology and increasing interdependence of business firms in the global scenario the manpower requirements of these industries have also changed. Industry requires people of totally different profile with very good technical knowledge, supported by managerial talent, attractive personality, good communication skills and better industry insight; if industries in fact search for people who can work with the global mindset.

This basically needs a different type of grooming of the commerce graduates inside and outside the classroom. This poses great challenge to faculty and institutions as well. Thus, in this backdrop efforts at different levels have been made to identify variety of parameters so that industry maintain close relationship and function in such an environment that helps each other in their operations.

Objectives

The main objectives of the present study are underlined below:

- To assess the present status of the subject under study.
- To find out ways as to how education – industry linkages can effectively be established.
- To offer suggestions for further improvement.

Methodology

The instructions in commerce in Jammu and Kashmir State is imparted in 20 colleges of which 09 are affiliated to the University of Jammu and the other 11 to the University of Kashmir. The information for the present analysis has been gathered on the basis of field study of all the colleges. A schedule spread over 10 parameters has been designed and responses gathered against each parameter analysed. An attempt has also been made to quantify the descriptive information by evaluating the performance under each parameter by assigning a score of 10 each.

Results and Discussions

The introspection of Table 5.1 reveals that the colleges engaged in commerce education in Jammu and Kashmir State in aggregate have been able to secure 20 per cent score only with regard to the corporate – academia interface.

The parameter wise analysis and discussion thereupon is detailed hereunder:

X1. Contributing articles on issues of importance to the industry by the faculty in journals published by corporate sector. The Jammu and Kashmir Bank Ltd., the only listed company in the Jammu and Kashmir State. The Banquest

(J&K Bank) is the only financial journal published in the state. It has been gathered that the faculty in the 4 colleges has started contributing papers in this journal with a special focus on the banking sector. Against 10 points, this parameter has obtained 2 points based on the content analysis of the journal.

Table 5.1:

Parameters	Scores	
	Standard	Performance
X1	10	2
X2	10	5
X3	10	X
X4	10	X
X5	10	2
X6	10	4
X7	10	X
X8	10	7
X9	10	X
X10	10	X
Total	**100**	**20**

X2. Organizing seminars/conferences and student centric programmes with industry sponsored by providing financial support. The Banks Federation Chamber of Industries Kashmir (FCIK), Kashmir Chamber of Commerce and Industries (KCCI), SMEs have been sponsoring various academic events organized in the colleges. The training programmes with special focus on 'Entrepreneurship Development' for students are also being conducted. This parameter has been in a position to obtain 5 points.

X3. Inviting entrepreneurs, practitioners and professionals to contribute articles in the journals published by the colleges. The professional journals are not yet published by all the colleges.

However, so far two professional journals namely:

(i) The Business Milieu; and

(ii) The Business Peep have been launched and some issues have already been released. But, the managers from the industry have not yet offered their contributions based on empirical evidences. As such this parameter has drawn blank in securing a point.

X4. Accommodating faculty on the Board of Directors. The practice of accommodation commerce faculty in the colleges on the Board of Directors of the corporates as independent directors has not yet been started. This parameter, therefore, has not scored any point.

X5. Conducting sessions by the faculty in the Corporate Training Institutes. The faculty members though limited in number are engaged in conducting such training sessions in the corporate training institutes for the corporate people. Two points have been scored under this parameter keeping in view the number of programmes conducted and the faculty engaged.

X6. Inviting guest speakers from the industry for lecturing and sharing their corporate experiences with the college students. The guest speakers are occasionally invited from the banks and insurance sectors besides professionals in the fields of Accounting and management engaged in the industry and also the successful entrepreneurs to discuss topical issues and share their experiences in the special programmes organized in this regard. Four points have been earned under this parameter with due cognizance of the frequency, guest faculty invited during academic sessions.

X7. Involving business managers in the curriculum development. The course structure and contents for the classes run in the colleges are designed by BOUS in the respective Universities. However, it has been a practice in the PG Department of Commerce, University of Kashmir that a workshop is organized by deliberating upon the course structure and course contents preceding

BOUS meeting. So far the people from industry have not been invited to contribute in such workshops. There are not people from the industry on the BOUS as well. However, people from the industry in future are expected to be engaged in the curriculum development. This parameter has thus failed to score any point.

X8. Organizing industrial tours for the students. The B.Com and BBA students within and outside the state. All the colleges imparting instructions in commerce are arranging industrial visits tours every year. This parameter, therefore, has scored the maximum 7 points.

X9. Arranging placement of students for training and recruitment in the industry. The placement cells have not been established in the colleges. The proper MOUs with the industry have not been executed to make the vocational programme in commerce effective. The failure of vocational programmes could partly be attributed to such drawback. Thus, no score has been made on this account.

X10. Launching of minor and major research projects by the industry for analysing problems confronting industry in its different functional areas and evaluating performance. The research projects major or minor have not been launched by the industry in the past. However, it is expected that proposals to this effect would be sent to the banks and SMEs by the faculty for their financial support. This parameter has also not been in a position to earn a score.

Conclusions

The study finally arrives at this conclusion that there is enough space created for furthering the bondage between the corporate and academia. The interface at present has been in a position to avail of scores to the extent of 20 per cent only. In all the parameters identified in the present study, the faculty in the academic institutions and business managers are required to come together so that the students who eventually form the human resource for the industry are properly groomed during their stay in the institutions.

REFERENCES

Agarwal, G. C. (1992), "Excellence in Business Education", Prof. A. Das Memorial Lecture, SLV All India Commerce Conference, University of Bangalore.

Agarwal, J. C. (1960), Teaching of Commerce: A Practical Approach, Vikas Publishing House Pvt. Ltd., New Delhi.

Fayyaz Ahmad, Sayyed (1998), Vocationsation of Business Education in India: Implementation, Constraints and Opportunities, *The Business Review*, 4(1&2): 11-20

Gilkar, Nazir Ahmad (2002), Commerce Education in Kashmir: A Study, Book Vision, Srinagar.

Prasad, J. (1993), "Stress on Skills" Business, Business India, Sept. 13-16.

Reddy, S. G. (2006), Industry Business Institute Interaction for Quality Management Education, University News.

Sharma, B.C. and Singh, W.C. (2007), "Re-defining Commerce Education in India, Arth Anvesan, 2(1): 31-34.

Tiwari, Arvind Kishore (2007), Industry-University/Business School Interaction for Quality Management/Commerce Education, in V. K. Singh (Edit), Innovations in Management Practices, Macmillan India Ltd.

UGC (1993), Vocationlisation of First Degree Education, New Delhi.

CHAPTER

6

Higher Education
Perspective of Quality Accounting Education

ABSTRACT

Accounting education and research continued to evolve in scope and academics and over the years made varied and substantial contribution towards its development. The discipline under its umbrella covers a variety of independent branches and other sub-branches are emerging significantly, and, thus, play a vital role in the restructuring of the industry and trade especially in the volatile business environment. Accordingly, shaping the vision envisages certain tangible competencies preferably IT based have to be built in the learners pursuing this branch of knowledge through designing compatible course structure. The curriculum has to be transacted beyond the normal classroom setting, through practical orientation in the industry and besides the traditional mode of instruction other delivery/evaluation methodologies offer enough scope for their application. Research in the area is being carried-on a Snail's pace which needs to gather momentum in a sustainable fashion. Accordingly, teachers have to frequently undergo faculty development programmes (RCS), gain practical exposure in industry and offer consultancy services. The present paper is a humble attempt towards this direction.

Introduction

Accounting – the language of business – is used to communicate multiple aspects of business operations. The days are gone when accounting was confined to record-keeping and compilation of final accounts only. However, accounting is much more extensive in its scope: designing a systems for classifying and summarising recorded data and interpreting them for internal and external users. The external-end users are essentially interested in the determination of profitability/ financial position. While as, the internal end-users emphasise on performance appraisal, business operations, decision-making, planning and so on (Bhattacharya, *et al*, 1984). Thus, accounting is now a distinctively identifiable discipline, which has continued to evolve, expand and diversify its coverage. The horizon of accounting education and research has extended scope-wise and lately information technology has revolutionalised its nature.

The discipline of accounting under its umbrella embraces a variety of branches like, Financial Accounting, Corporate Accounting, Cost Accounting, Management Accounting and Tax Accounting. The other sub-branches (*viz*.: Environment Accounting, Inflation Accounting, Human Resource Accounting, Public Interest Accounting, Brand Accounting, etc.,) have emerged significantly and new directions have, thus, been given to the process. Of late, the discipline has gained keen interest among academics, as a sequel to it a variety of contributions over the years emerged covering different dimensions. The environment of business, on the other hand, is highly volatile and ever changing. Thus, Nikam (1999), realises the need for reshaping of accounting education and profession so as to enable the students to face the challenges and to enjoy opportunities created in the present millennium. Azam (1999) evaluates the business environment in operation today, forecasts business needs for tomorrow and, accordingly, assesses infrastructure for accounting teaching to bridge the gaps and finally suggests some proactive measures for improving the discipline to meet the challenges posed to the business by ever changing business environment. Sharma (1997) states that globalisation posed a challenging situation to accounting education and research. The future accountants, as such, are required to develop the capacity for enquiry, logical thinking and critical analysis. The curriculum management, accordingly, has to be restructured.

The Study

Rationale

The phenomenal change at global level as a result of LPG, with emphasis on IT has revolutionised thinking all over the world. Thus, in view of the changing profile of the Indian economy under WTO regime, the quality assurance in accounting education assumes an added significance in this context. 'But, the delivery in accounting education in operation is mainly based on lecture mode of instruction and chalk and talk method, Similarly, the evaluation of the learner performance vis-a-vis the preset objectives rests on the terminal examinations. The research, which is an essential ingredient so necessary for keeping teaching alive, is still sporadic among teachers engaged in the teaching of accounting. The faculty development programmes (RCs) are rarely organized in accounting discipline separately and the faculty, in general, have a least industrial exposure. The consultancy services too are offered at a small scale, Thus, in view of the aforesaid backdrop the present study peeps into invisibility.

Objectives

The specific objective of the present paper is to assess the current operational dimensions and future demands of the accounting education under the changing global economic scenario.

Methodology

The study is based on the available literature, and expert views of the professionals and academics in the area gathered during interaction sessions arranged for the purpose. The present exploratory study is also supplemented by empirical evidences gathered through conducting a preparatory workshop exercise attended by teachers engaged in the teaching of accounting and research activities in the colleges affiliated to the University of Kashmir. Respondents marked their responses to the observations schedule containing varied dimensions (25 items) on 5 point Likert type scale of measurement weighted; thus, Rl (very important) = 5, R2 (important) = 3 and R3 (not much important) = l. The responses gathered have been classified under five broad categories each accommodating 5 items and accordingly, tabulated to facilitate analysis. The ranks assigned to each dimension under a specific category have been based on total weighted score (TWS) and average weighted score (AWS), thus obtained. The first draft of the paper was also presented in this workshop and respondents discussed and commented on its different aspects. The collective wisdom of the participants, in the final analysis, guided towards affecting healthy changes in the draft paper.

Results and Discussion

The analysis made in Table 6.1 is in support of studying various sub-accounting branches under an independent branch of accounting as this dimension has scored the highest TWS (198). The emerging sub areas are required to be developed fully so as to enjoy a distinct and independent accounting branch and, thus, captioned as "Issue based Accounting? The details are given in Fig. 6.1. The All India Accounting Association (AIAA) is required to ensure that the UGC and Professional institutes maintain an integration and, at least, one common core of study preferably on issue based accounting, as discussed above, covering all emerging sub areas, is designed and adopted by all the Universities and institutes engaged in the teaching of accounting. Steps are also to be initiated to exchange teachers from university/college departments frequently to the institutes and vice versa. This mutually beneficial relationship, thus, worked out between professional bodies and Universities, would help in reshaping

Table 6.1: Accounting Branches

S. No.	Items	Responses (%)			TWS	AWS	Rank
		R1	R2	R3			
1.	Developing emerging sub areas (grouped under an independent branch as 'Issue based Accounting'	87.5	10.0	2.5	198.0	4.95	I
2.	Exchanging teachers from academic centres to professional institutions and vice versa (for benefit of the faculty as well as the discipline)	85.0	10.0	5.0	184.0	4.60	II
3.	Developing a core course of study (of all accounting programmes covering issue based accounting)	80.0	12.5	7.5	178.0	4.45	III
4.	Searching an answer for instructional/evaluation strategies (for transacting syllabi through other than lecture method.)	75.0	17.5	7.5	174.0	4.35	IV
5.	Operating curricular activities in accordance with well designed teaching plans (administered in the beginning of the academic session)	72.5	17.5	10.0	170.0	4.25	V
	Average across all items	80.0	13.5	6.5	180.8	3.52	

and enriching the course structure in this discipline after a thorough review. The focus of the whole exercise has to be on developing the practical competencies apart from required conceptual and numerical skills among the students. Such an institutional linkage at the international level is also essential in our wider interest. The transaction of the prescribed syllabi is required to travel beyond the four walls of the normal class room setting; thus, kept open for other windows of teaching as well. In this regard a set of 25 instructional methodologies befitting the discipline has been identified and given in Fig. 6.2.

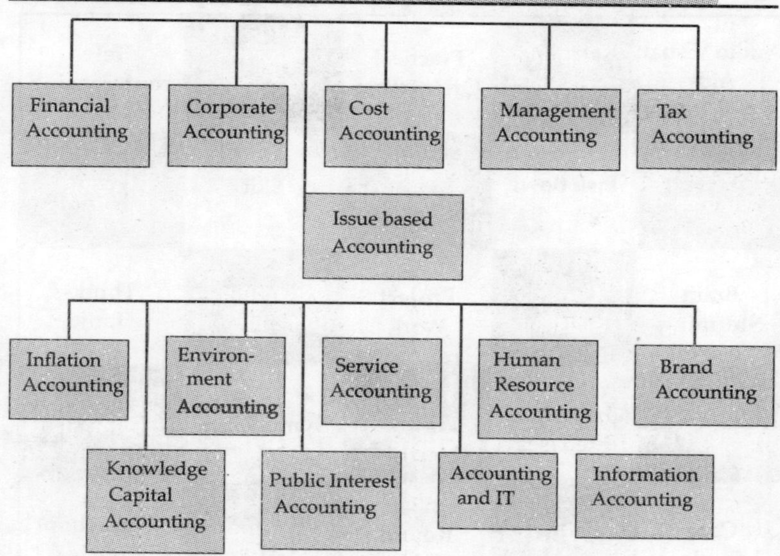

Fig. 6.1: Accounting Branches

A variety of methods has also to be put into operation for assessing the performance and home take knowledge of the students vis-a-vis the preset objectives. The Curriculum Evaluation strategies are reflected in Fig. 6.3. The evaluation reports of the student performance in the term end examination have to be analysed/published and for every examination the standard answer sheets question-wise are made available for the guidance of the students pursuing a specific course of study in accounting education. This exercise will orient students as to how effectively respond to a particular problem. The well designed teaching plans are to be made available to the students, at the commencement of the session, embodying various elements of syllabi as well as the specific teaching methodology to be adopted component-wise under each unit.

The study under Table 6.2, prioritises with Rank-I, the identification of specific delivery/evaluation modes course content-wise. The transacting of a particular content of curriculum in different accounting branches has to be effected

Audio Visual Aids	Debate Session	Practical Orientation	Students Portfolio	Tele-conferencing
Accounting Games	Fish Bowl	Panel Discussions	Skit	T-Groups
Brain Storming	Group Discussions	Project Work	Seminar Presentation	Think-Tank
Buzz Sessions	Inbasket Exercises	Role Play	Symposium	Tutorials
Case Study	Lecture/ Discussion	Round Table	Syndicate Method	Workshop Exercise

Fig. 6.2: Curriculum Transaction Strategies

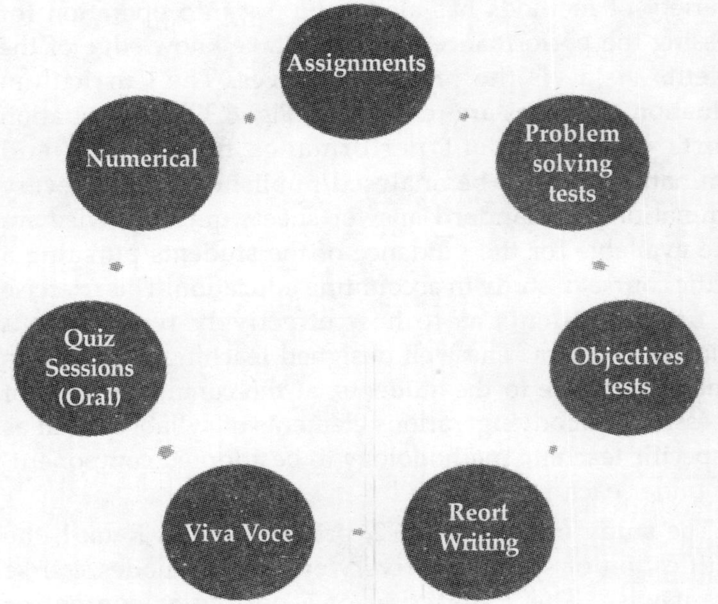

Fig. 6.3: Curriculum Evaluation Strategies

Table 6.2: Curriculum Management

S. No.	Items	Responses (%)			TWS	AWS	Rank
		R1	R2	R3			
1.	Identifying specific delivery/evaluation modes (for each course content in every accounting branch)	95.0	2.5	2.5	194.0	4.85	I
2.	Organizing workshops on methodology of accounting Research (for orienting with the latest trends in accounting research)	90.0	7.5	2.5	190.0	4.75	II
3.	Sponsoring Research projects – major as well as minor – on accounting issues (for analysing issues confronting industry)	87.5	10.0	2.5	188.0	4.70	III
4.	Setting up fully equipped accounting labs (documentation as well as networking connectivity-wise)	82.5	12.5	5.0	182.0	4.55	IV
5.	Organizing remedial coaching classes and holding special session (for students weak in accounting and gifted students motivating them to pursue profe-ssional accounting programme)	75.0	20.0	5.0	176.0	4.40	V
	Average across all items	86.0	10.5	3.5	186.0	4.65	

in accordance with some specific delivery strategies together with evaluation mechanism, which have been worked out and details are highlighted in Fig. 6.4. The launching of an accounting lab-fully equipped with the documentation and network connectivity is now the need of the hour.

S. No.	Course Content	Methodology		Evaluation
		Accounting Branches	Delivery	
1.	Concept Dissemination	All Accounting Branches	Lecture/ Discussion	Viva-Voce
2.	Standard Costing	Management Accounting	Role Play	Oral Presentation
3.	Banking Company Accounts	Corporate Accounting	Practical Orientation	Problem Solving Tests
4.	Reconciliation of Profits (Cost *v/s* Finance)	Cost Accounting	Debate Sessions	Numerical Analysis
5.	Insurance Claims Settlement	Financial Accounting	Round Table	Objective Tests (True/False
6.	Tax Assessment (Salary)	Tax Accounting	Case Study	Numerical Analysis
7.	Financial Statement Analysis	Financial Accounting	Buzz Session	Quiz Session (Oral)
8.	Tax Planning (Saving Schemes)	Tax Accounting	Seminar Present-ation	Objective Tests (Multiple choice)
9.	Break-Even Analysis	Management Accounting	Accounting Games	Assignments
10.	Cost Sheet	Cost Accounting	Student Portfolio	Report Wiring

Fig. 6.4: Course-wise Delivery/Evaluation Methodology

The teaching departments in the Colleges/Universities are, thus, required to tie up with the industry and taxation departments, in order to acquire their annual corporate reports, annual operational plans, newsletters, performance reports, sales tax/income tax returns etc., for the in-house training of the students in the laboratory. It is in place to state that the significance of accounting standards, forming a component of any accounting course structure, can't be undermined. Also, the globalisation being in process, a need for commonly accepted uniform accounting standards is felt urgently. Thus, steps need be initiated to lay hands on the Corporate Annual Reports with the objective to explain the conceptual framework, under the changing paradigm, with the help of empirical evidences. The academically fragile learners are to be taken care of and their deficiencies made up by organizing 'Remedial Coaching Sessions', yet the gifted students, after the process of admission for B. Com courses in the college sector is completed need to be are searched for by conducting rigorous screening tests and a group of students, thus, identified having their aptitude for professional programmes in accounting (*viz.*: ICAI, ICWAI, ICSI, IFCAI, etc.), are groomed and accordingly, made competent enough to pursue a desired programme after acquiring the first degree. The college sector offers B. Com (General), B. Com (Hons) and B. Com (Vocational) progammes. The (identified group of students will undergo rigorous training especially in accounting papers during their three year stay in the college. The research projects – major as well as minor – have to be offered by the professional bodies/research institutes, university departments/industry etc., on important accounting issues in close alliance with the business centres involving professionals, practitioners and academics jointly or independently to carryout such projects. This way a space will be provided to motivate researchers to undertake research projects in the area of accounting education. Again, the findings of such research projects should also be shared by way of paper contributions in the seminars/conferences and writing of monographs, books etc. Further, a series of workshops on 'Methodology for Accounting Research' should be organized by the university departments jointly with the professional institutions, so that the researchers in this discipline are equipped with the relevant tools and techniques enabling them to identity, understand, analyse, discuss and handle research problems properly.

The introspection of Table 6.3 reflects that placement of teachers in the industry has scored the highest AWS (4.90) against the AWS of all items (4.75). The steps are, thus to be initiated for the placement of teachers engaged in the accounting education in the industry for some period of time preferably during summer/winter vacations enabling them to work on projects to understand the accounting mechanism in operation and analyse a particular accounting problem confronting the enterprise.

Table 6.3: Faculty Development

S. No.	Items	Responses (%)			TWS	AWS	Rank
		R1	R2	R3			
1.	Arranging placement of teachers in industry (for some period during summer/winter vacations)	95.0	5.0	–	196.0	4.90	I
2.	Organizing RCs in Commerce (focus on accounting education and research)	92.5	5.0	2.5	192.4	4.80	II
3.	Conducting FDPs for teachers engaged in teaching of accounting (focus on different accounting branches)	90.0	7.5	2.5	190.0	4.75	III
4.	Supporting faculty to present papers in national/international seminars/conferences organized by accounting bodies (focus on interaction with others in order to gain exposure)	87.5	10.0	2.5	188.0	4.70	IV
5.	Encouraging faculty for publishing research papers on emerging accounting issues (focus on dissemination of research findings)	85.0	10.0	5.0	184.0	4.60	V
	Average across all items	90.0	7.5	2.5	190.0	4.75	

The improvement in the quality of accounting education necessitates appropriate training and practical orientation to the concerned teachers. The AIAA is required to tie up with the University where the annual conference of the association is held to organize FDP (RC) on accounting for the benefit of teachers and this has to be a regular annual feature. Further, ASCs under the UGC Scheme of faculty development in different Universities are required to arrange RCS in Accounting in their normal schedule of business. It is essential that the faculty is supported in their endeavours to write papers on important themes and present and defend the same in the national/international seminars, conferences. Thus, share ideas and interact with their professional colleagues in order to gain exposure. Further, the research papers shall also be published on the emerging accounting issues to identify the frontiers and disseminate the findings of the research both conceptual and empirical.

The investigation attempted in Table 6.4 highlights that tripolar interface in accounting education has been assigned Rank-I. The triangular interface affected among University-institution-industry would ultimately result in the improvement in the accounting education and research. The Accounting Clubs have to be established for promoting the culture of holding Seminars, debates, group discussions, etc. These clubs should also be authorised to arrange Guest lectures, on the latest developments in accounting, by eminent scholars, professional accountants, legal luminaries, leading entrepreneurs, etc. The student Career Counselling/Placement Centres have to be established with a view to guide students in both the areas of academic advancement and the job opportunities. The student placement cells, thus, have to take charge of;

1. Training and placement of students in the corporate sector.
2. Field trips and industrial visits of the students; and
3. Visits to institutes of excellence.

The Internal Quality Control Cells (IQCC) have to be established with a view to ensure quality accounting education.

Also to monitor academic activities of the key players (*viz.*: teachers and students) to ensure efficacy in the educational system *viz.*:

(i) Controlling student absenteeism.

(ii) Strengthening teacher-student interaction especially off the classroom session.

(iii) Effective performance evaluation of the teachers by the students.

(iv) Contributions of the teachers in the research journals and writing books.

(v) Monitoring the performance vis-a-vis preset objectives.

Table 6.4: Innovative Initiatives

S. No.	Items	Responses (%)			TWS	AWS	Rank
		R1	R2	R3			
1.	Effecting triangular interface (focus on academic-institution-industry interface)	95.0	2.5	2.5	194.0	4.85	I
2.	Creating Quality Assurance Cell (for ensuring TQM in accounting education and research)	90.0	7.5	2.5	190.0	4.75	II
3.	Setting up Career Counselling/Placement Centres (for guiding of students)	87.5	10.0	2.5	188.0	4.70	III
4.	Arranging utility based capsule programmes (for non-accounting keeping entrepreneurs)	85.0	10.0	5.0	184.0	4.60	IV
5.	Establishing Accounting Clubs at University/College/Institution level (for organizing seminars/debates etc.)	82.5	12.5	5.0	182.0	4.55	V
	Average across all items	86.0	8.5	3.5	187.6	4.70	

The steps are required to be initiated to design capsule courses in Accounting for non-accounting knowing entrepreneurs enabling them to maintain accounting records, which are to be utilised for the purpose of taxation and analysis of operational results of their enterprises. The college/ University departments should offer consultancy and accounting services to the small traders/manufacturers especially in the VAT and GST regime. The services of the pass-outs yet unemployed can be utilised for maintaining and compiling accounts of such small business enterprises. This exercise will prove a win-win situation for both the traders and the unemployed youth trained in account keeping as well.

The securitisation of Table 6.5 reveals that the promoting awareness in e-Accounting for both candidates as well as corporate has been assigned preference with the highest response (Rl = 97.50%). The traditional accounting system has now been rendered obsolete and the impact of IT on accounting education has bound to be phenomenal and manifold. The streamlining of accounting system under new framework has dispensed drudgetary of conventional files and correspondence 'with office automation. Accordingly, the need of the hour is to train students in the lately developed accounting packages. The developing of adequate skills in e-Accounting with a view to create a niche in the IT enabled corporate sector to open employment avenues for the numerous degree holders in the accounting discipline. The setting-up of training institutes with job specific centres has also gained an added importance for meeting the market demand. The off-shoring was bound to play an important role in securing high value added jobs. It had resulted in higher growth and led to new employment opportunities. The global volume of the off-shoring market was in the range of $10 billion to $50 billion. India is a mother country of off shore outsourcing. Costs have been the only irritant, but availability of skilled staff in abundance is another contribution. Thus, to maximize gains of off shoring, a better course of action could be to field as many winners as possible (Hindu,

2004). An immediate need is to promote awareness in c-Accounting involving candidates as well as corporates. Thus, for meeting market demand for people, the institutions set-up are required to focus on specific training courses covering basic computer skills, internet with high speed connectivity etc. A good number of positions are expected to be available in the world. So the students are to be equipped with the desired skills as may make them competent enough to get a suitable job in the market. Thus, to have B.Com+ and M.Com++ degree so that these degree holders enjoy competitive edge in the job market.

Table 6.5: E-Accounting

S. No.	Items	Responses (%)			TWS	AWS	Rank
		R1	R2	R3			
1.	Promoting awareness in e-Accounting (for both candidates as well as corporate)	97.5	2.5	–	198.0	4.95	I
2.	Setting up training institutes with job specific centres for meeting the market demand)	95.0	5.0	–	196.0	4.90	II
3.	Developing adequate skills in E-Accounting (for B.Com and M.Com degree holders)	92.5	7.5	–	194.0	4.85	III
4.	Creating a niche in the world IT enabled corporate sector (for the target skill bore of B.Com and M.Com degree holders)	90.0	7.5	2.5	189.0	4.73	IV
5.	Creating employment opportunities (for numerous unemployed B.Com and M.Com degree holders)	87.5	10.0	2.5	186.0	4.65	V
	Average across all items	92.5	6.5	1.0	192.6	4.82	

Conclusions

The emerging issues have to be grouped together to constitute an identifiable accounting branch; thus, studied as such under 'Contemporary Issues in Accounting'. The faculty shall necessarily have an industrial exposure and academic-institution-industry interface to strengthen the conceptual and application blending. Towards the quality assurance, instruction is required to be improved by employing newer and innovative modes of delivery supplemented by effective evaluation mechanism with focus on research activities.

REFERENCES

Agarwal, A. G. (1994), "Role of Management Accountant in Liberalised Economy". *The Management Accountant,* 29(9): 650-652.

Azam, M. K. (1999), "Proactive Approach to Accounting Education", *The Management Accountant,* 34(5): 371-372.

Bhatcharya, *et al.* (1984), "Accounting for Managers", Vani Educational Books, New Delhi.

Hindu (2004), "Outsourcing will Enhance Job Prospects", News Item; Oct. 21: 18.

Nikam, R. S, (1999), "Some Emerging Issues in Accounting Education and Profession", *The Indian Journal of Commerce,* 54(4): 20.

Shankaran, Scncider and Douglas (1991), "Preparation of Accounting Graduates for Professional Accounting Career in the USA". Chartered Accountant, XXXX(9): 564-567.

CHAPTER

7

Higher Education

Operational Aspects of Reforming Examinations

Introduction

The term 'examination' derived from the Latin word 'examen' means the tongue of a balance. Examinations, thus, have definite functions – systematically test the knowledge and skills acquired by the students, assess the efficiency of the teachers and perform 'diagnostic' as well as 'prognostic' operations. Accordingly, examinations are of varied types – written or practical, and external or internal – depending on the controlling authority (Bhatia and Bhatia, 1994).

The Study

Need

From time to time various steps have been initiated by the concerned to streamline the examination system. The causes as to why examination system suffers a setback demand an indepth study. The probable factors, thus, could be:

(a) The examination process has become a victim of operational inefficiencies and unfair practices.

(b) The testing tools have turned blunt and deficient in the changing educational scenario.

(c) The education system itself is confronting with certain constraints, the impact of which ultimately is reflected on the examinations.

(d) The examination system is revisited for its up-gradation when other components of the curriculum management exhibit better performance.

The main objective of viable examination system has been to affect an improvement in the standards of education. Accordingly, the present paper has been attempted to study the factors that demand an improvement in the management of examinations.

Objectives

The paper pursues the following specific objectives:

- To identify the problem areas.
- To suggest the remedial initiatives.

Methodology

The information for analysis has been gathered from the relevant notifications issued by the concerned academic bodies. The paper covers the study of first degree level examinations and is based on the observations of the author.

Analysis and Discussion

Problem Areas

- The academic calendar, instructional days available per academic session, contact hours per week, etc., are some of the essential aspects in evaluating the teaching-learning process. The NAAC Peer Teams during their academic audit of the college sector here in the valley, accordingly focused on these aspects and observed that the days available for transaction have fallen short of 180 during an academic session as prescribed by the University Grants Commission (Fig. 7.1). This state of affairs inter alia has been ascribed to the longer period of time consumed in the conduct of annual examinations and the declaration of results there of.

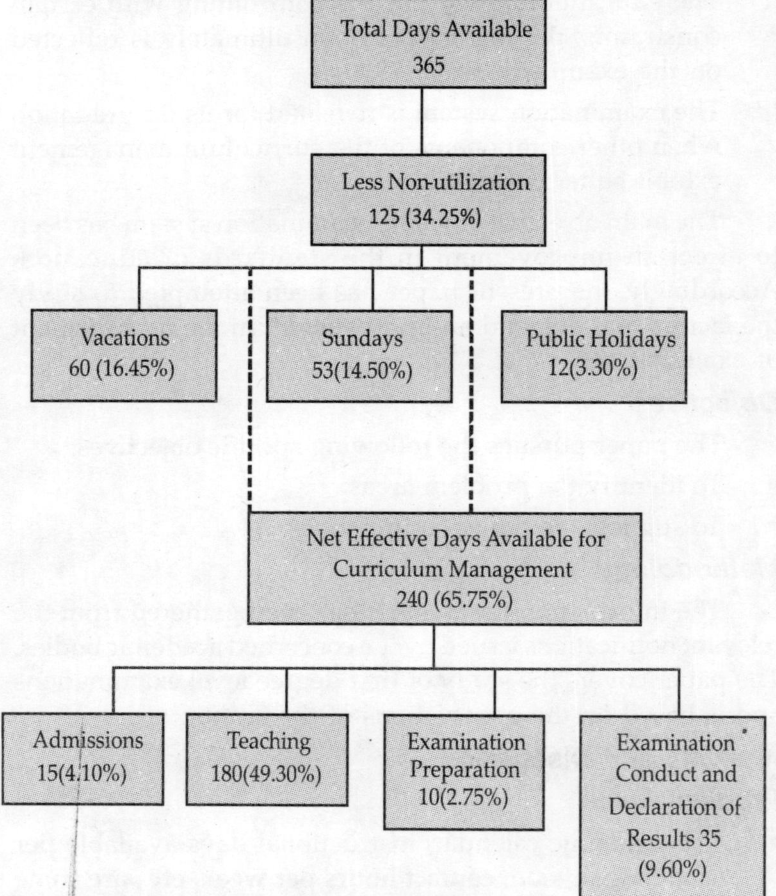

Fig. 7.1: Benchmark Operational Cycle

Note: Figures within parentheses indicate percentage.
Source: Based on the UGC Notification on 'Measures for the Maintenance of Standards, 1998, p. 13.

- The fact is evidenced by the analysis of data that this annual ritual called examinations has been too lengthy a process has consumed a precious period of time. The BG year end examinations have been spread over a long period as the examinations cycle right from the day first of the examinations until the declaration of their results by the University has been very wide. The average period consumed for the conduct of examinations has been 45 days in the range of 41 days and 52 days. Also the average operational performance cycle of examinations has been 131 days in the range of 92 days and 154 days (Table 7.1). Against the UGC norms, the adverse variances, thus, registered for the 1st year, 2nd year and 3rd year examinations have been 113, 119,57 days respectively (Table 7.2).

Table 7.1: Performance Operational Cycle (Session 2004-05 Annual)

Year	Conduct			Result Preparation		Performance Cycle (Days)
	Begin	End	Total Days	Results Declared	Total Days	
BG I	4th Nov. 04	14th Dec. 04	41 days	31st Mar 05	107 days	148 days
BG II	27th Dec. 04	16th Feb. 05	52 days	28th May, 05	102 days	154 days
BG III	30th Nov. 04	11th Jan 05	43 days	1st Mar., 05	49 days	92 days
Avg.			45 days		80 days	131 days

Source: Based on Data Sheets and Result Notifications.

Table 7.2: Variance Analysis

Year	Examination Cycle (Days)			Activity Based Analysis
	Benchmark	Performance	Variance Adverse	
BG I	35	148	(113)	
BG II	35	154	(119)	
BG III	35	92	(57)	
Avg.	35	131	(96)	

Source: Based on Data Sheets and Result Notifications.

- The question papers cover stereotype and repetitive questions are asked generally. Whereas, various other tests like objective are not utilised. The examinees rely on the shortcuts and guess questions. The examination system banks heavily on rote memory and, as such, hardly induces students to think, analyse, debate and discuss a particular problem. Again, the practice of 'Note Dictation' promotes only students dependency on the teachers. The entire gamut of education has finally been examination oriented. As a sequel to it, the general depth of knowledge has suffered mainly as a result of selective and superficial studies. Further, the course structure especially in the social sciences accommodates too many course combinations. The course load has not evenly been distributed across all the three years at the undergraduate programme. Added to this, the annual examinations lead to hard work at the fag end of the year which results into the strain and stress and adversely affects both the physical and mental health of the students.
- The adequate care is not taken in paper setting and marking answer scripts. Construction of questions is not keeping up with a well developed assessment scheme. Voices are echoed regarding partialities exercised in awarding marks in examinations. Complaints of prior leakage of the question papers have generally been observed. Further, the students avail of no opportunities to discuss their examination results with their teachers. Also results are not used to offer a feedback for improvement in the process of teaching-learning. Adequate heed is also not paid towards Date sheet preparation.

Remedial Initiatives

The remedial initiatives are based on the under scored premises:

(i) That all the components of curriculum management (*viz.*: course planning, development, transaction and evaluation) are accorded a fair level play.

(ii) That all the stake holders in the educational process exhibit seriousness of purpose and sincerity to the mission in maintaining the efficacy of the examination system. Thus, the following remedial initiatives are expected to give a turn around to the examination system through operational effectiveness of the system.

- The existing over-emphasis on annual examinations needs to be minimized and, accordingly, a due reliance has to be placed on the term based examinations. The academic session, in the aforesaid backdrop, is required to be divided into two terms. Term-1 may cover all the 'A' papers and, thus, the examination for this term is to be held in the second fortnight of July. The University is desired to set the examination papers and fix the examination schedule with a view to maintain uniformity. However, the concerned teachers have to be assigned the task of marking the answer scripts, compilation of award sheets preferably during their leisure time in the college. The Examination Committees at each college, thus, will co-ordinate this exercise under the supervision of concerned Principal and dispatch the Result Performance Sheets of this term to the Controller of Examinations in the University. However, adequate checks and balances are to be exercised in this regard. The University as per the practice in vogue will organize the examination for 'B' papers only in each subject/module during the second fortnight of December every year (Table 7.3). Thus, the final results, for all the classes are expected to be made public by the University latest by the first week of February every year enabling the colleges to complete the process of admissions, classifications, academic map (time table), etc., by the end of February every year. The BOSE results for Higher Secondary Part-ll are also expected to be available by the end of January every year and the admission formalities for the 1st, 2nd and 3rd years are to be completed by the end of February in order to ensure commencement of the academic session on the 1st March with the regular transaction of academic work that entails the entire gamut of teaching – learning activities.

Table 7.3: Term-wise Scheme

	Term-I (March-July)	Term-II (Aug-Dec.)	Academic Session
Available Days (Agg.) Excluding Winter Vacations)	151	153	304
Non-utilisation (I + II)	41	50	91
- Sundays/Holidays	41	40	81
- Summer Vacations	–	10	10
Available days (net)	110	103	213
- For Transaction	90	90	180
- For Exam. Preparations	05*	05	10
- For Examination conduct	15	08	23

Term-II Examinations can be extended for 7 more days of January.

- The University may declare results faculty-wise (*viz.*: Sciences, Social Sciences, Home Sciences, Business Sciences) as and when ready; rather, wait for the finalisation of the results in respect of all the examinations/ programme. This practice will offer a double advantage:
  - *(a)* to evenly distribute the heavy rush of students seeking admissions in the colleges for BG ll and BG lll years; and
  - *(b)* to effect economy in the days consumed in the process of admissions. The Model Plan for Examination Operations (Date Sheet) is given in Table 7.4.
- The current century has created a new educational environment and people talk about 'borderless education'. The GATS under WTO regime leads to a global level competition and global mobility of students' demands sustenance of quality in higher education in particular. Thus, there is no scope for limited studies or selective coverage of syllabi under the paradigm where the students have to be globally competitive. The evaluation simply is one of the components of curriculum management and,

as such, the whole educational process has not to be subordinated to the examinations. The practice is to declare a particular portion of the syllabi the most or the least important from the examination stand point during the course of teaching is to be discarded.

Table 7.4: Plan for Examination Operations (PEO) – Data Sheet

Features	Comments
Equity • A variety of courses of study, like core, vocational, operational find a place in the course portfolio of different disciplines • The courses of study are also Hard as well as Soft • The PEO is, thus required to provide equal opportunities to all the examinees intra as well as inter faculty for their preparations during the intervening period of examination papers.	
Timing • The detailed plan for academic as well as teaching operations are formulated and made available to the students at the commencement of session. • The other components of the curriculum management, *viz.*: course designing, course transaction are also decided well in advance. • The similar treatment is desired and deserved to be accorded to the PEO, which is also a component of curriculum management	

In Sum

The aforesaid discussion is expected to result in, thus:

- To effect economy in the days consumed during the process of examinations and declaration of results.
- To ensure that the required days as envisaged by the UGC are made available for the syllabi transaction in accordance with the teaching plans designed in the beginning of each term.
- To outsource certain other examination oriented activities by the University to the college sector.
- To pave a step towards academic autonomy to be enjoyed by the college institutions.
- To relieve students of the stress and other vagaries of the annual examinations.
- To discourage large scale absenteeism in the colleges.
- To stimulate seriousness in studies by the students.
- To promote true academic culture in the colleges.
- To avoid the practice of making studies examination oriented.
- To operationalise scope for the construction of multi-dimensional question papers.
- To exercise effective checks in respect of unfair practices, whatsoever in order to restore the efficiency and sanctity of examinations.
- To effect serious efforts at the hands of the teachers in preparing composite teaching and evaluation operational plans after analysing each unit of the syllabus with regard to every course of study.
- To create an atmosphere of genuine teacher – taught relationship wherein syllabus of each course of study is completed well in time to the satisfaction of students.
- To conduct tests frequently in order to keep the students fully engrossed in their studies.
- To constitute a study group of experts to look into the feasibility of narrowing down of the examination cycle

through minimizing the course combinations especially in the social sciences.

- To design Date Sheets providing equal opportunities to all the students in all the disciplines for their preparations.
- To initiate steps with a view to reduce the time lag between the conduct of examinations and the declaration of results by drawing a fixed examination schedule well in advance consisting of all activities.
- To frame a state level educational policy to provide a guidance in all the educational affairs including examinations.
- To make available in the college libraries the question papers in sets of the prior years (discipline-wise and year-wise) with a view to offer an opportunity to the students to have a look at the construction of questions.
- To settle the financial and other allied matters relating to examinations on priority basis, *viz.:*
    - compensating adequately the convenors of the Examination Committees in the colleges for their work;
    - submitting examination bills to the University through the offices of the Principal under proper receipt issued by the University;
    - collecting unconsumed material by the University in accordance with the schedule to be notified in the Date Sheet of each examination;
    - issuing NDC's to the examination centres within a week after the termination of examinations;
    - settling examination bills within a fortnight after the declaration of results;
    - clarifying the criterion for the appointment of first supervisor after the appointment of Deputy Superintendents;
    - implementing in letter and spirit the agreement with regard to the advance payment of 75 per cent.

REFERENCES

Bhatia and Bhatia (1994), The Principles and Methods of Teaching, Doba House Publishers, Delhi.

Gilkar, N. A. (2004), "Streamlining the Examination System", Greater Kashmir, Dec. 10, p. 7.

CHAPTER

8

Higher Education

Evaluation Study of Commerce Curriculum

ABSTRACT

The fast changing global business environment characterised by borderless world where in free flow of capital and technology has become a real phenomena. The preponderance of this surging phenomena of globalisation of businesses is huge and has necessitated an urgent need to train people professionally to manage this paradigm shift successfully. Training and equipping people with relevant skills comes under the gamut of academics. And commerce stream in academics is that branch of knowledge which produce the relevant people for managing this changed business scenario. Accordingly, the curriculum in Commerce needs constant restructuring with an objective to re-orient it according to the current needs. Curriculum, it is not only designing courses of study, but the process of curriculum management is a composite of four components like *(i)* curriculum planning, *(ii)* curriculum development, *(iii)* curriculum transaction and *(iv)* curriculum evaluation. The subject matter of curriculum is, undoubtedly, large and, as such, the study of present paper has be pruned to the last but important component *i.e.*, curriculum evaluation.

Introduction

In early 90's it was felt that Commerce and business studies curriculum must focus on business skills and application orientation keeping in view the changing economic scenario in the country. Accordingly, workshop on 'Reorientation of Commerce curriculum' was organized under the auspices of the University Department of Commerce on 30th June, 1994 and threadbare discussions were held based on the background paper presented on the occasion. Consequent upon the recommendations of the workshop, the BOUS in Commerce finally approved the course structure that was operational for the academic sessions 1996-2000. One of the vital development made was the addition of five compulsory course in each year of 3 year integrated B. Com degree programme and each year had in all six commerce courses including one optional under revised scheme. Some of the important courses in the existing syllabi were retained after updating and enrichment, as for instance 'Financial Accounting' paper incorporated international Accounting Standards. Irrelevant and obsolete courses were scrapped and a number of new courses like Computer Applications in Businesses, Economic Environment of Business, Business Mathematics, Project Report, Entrepreneurship Development were introduced. (The BR, Vol. 1, 1995). The students were required to qualify all the papers individually and with the passage of time it was found that commerce students were put to a disadvantageous position as against science and Arts students who have to qualify four subjects with A and B papers. Moreover, the economic environment of business is fast changing, so there was no scope for a static commerce curriculum. The courses which enjoyed an association with real life problems and practices and also necessary for industrial and economic development formed an integral part of the Commerce curriculum. Accordingly, a series of curriculum Review and Revision Sessions were organized during academic session 2000 and after studying its pros and cons, the BOUS in Commerce finally approved the course structure which now has been in operation from the academic session 2001 under which the courses were classified in four modules with A and B papers at each level of B. Com degree programme and the students were required to qualify each module separately. Further, teaching – learning process need to become more interactive with the use of innovative pedagogical techniques. The entire process need, thus, shed its passivity and become more learner centric. Supplementing lectures with other learner centred teaching is also a requirement under NAAC (Refer to Benchmark criterion ll (5). The format of question papers in vogue in commerce and business studies is traditional and covers one particular form questions, fewer in number limited in content of syllabi and sometimes construction of questions is vague. Accordingly, the focus of the present paper has been on:

- Assessing the process of curriculum planning and development.
- Examining the curriculum evaluation practices.
- Suggesting measures for improvement in curriculum management.

Discussions

Analysis

An attempt has been made to analyse some question papers. In this regard two question papers (Nov-Dec 2001 Session) were analysed. 'Financial Accounting' paper made a shift from the routine as each question was divided into two parts with their respective weightages. Under part *(a)* the conceptual understanding was tested and part *(b)* related to the application of accounting treatment for particular business transactions. The practice in science and social sciences has been exploited to the fullest use in the discipline of Commerce and business studies. Similarly, 'Business Statistics' paper gave more coverage to conceptual understanding; rather the application of statistical techniques shown in the Tables 8:1 and 8.2 given below:

Table 8.1: Analysis of Question Paper on Business Statistics

Number of Questions	Answer Required	Weightage	
		New	Old
Numerical Questions	Application of Statistical Techniques	10%	50%
Direct Theoretical Questions	Text Book Answer	50%	20%
Statement Type Questions	Text Book Answer	10%	10%
Case Study Type	Survey Application Oriented answer	10%	Nil
Conceptual with Numerical Overtones	Text Book Answer Theoretical with Numerical Blending	20%	30%

Source: Question papers on business statistics (old and new scheme) Nov-Dec. 2002.

Table 8.2: Analysis of Result Performance – Business Statistics

Old Scheme			New Scheme			Scheme-wise Ratio (Old: New)
Marks Obtained (%)	Range (%)	No. of Students (%)	Marks obtained	Range (5)	No. of Students	
Under Bottomline						
Less than 36	4-31	30(25)	Less than 27	10-24	61(44)	1:1.76
On the Bottomline						
36	–	21(17)	27	–	21(15)	1:0.88
Above the Bottomline						
37-59	37-59	61(51)	28-44	28-44	54(39)	1:0.76
60 and above	60-77	9(7)	45 and above	46-55	3(2)	1:0.28
Total			**120(100)**		**139(100)**	

Table 8.1: Analysis of question paper on business statistics.

Note:
- Figures within parentheses indicate percentage.
- Minimum marks obtained (% age) Old (4%) New (13%).
- Minimum marks obtained (% age) Old (77%) New 73%).

The analysis reveals that numerical questions requiring application of statistical techniques accounted for 10 per cent only as against 50 per cent under old scheme. Direct theoretical questions which need text book answers weighted for 50 per cent and 20 per cent respectively. Further, the analysis reveals that in business Statistics Paper against 25 per cent (old scheme), 44 per cent students (New scheme) bracketed themselves under the bottom line; whereas 15 per cent students in the latter as against 17 per cent of their counterparts were on the bottom line by obtaining minimum pass marks as required under University statutes 2 per cent and 7 per cent of the sample obtained 15* division under new and old scheme respectively. Finally in the new scheme 56 per cent students against 75 per cent of their counterparts passed this course of reading. However, under old scheme, marks obtained by examinees offered a wide spread range from 4-77 per cent whereas under new scheme comparatively ranged narrower as between 13-73 per cent. Large content of numerical questions proved an advantage for the students to pass the old scheme as against their counterparts in the new scheme. The need, thus, is to have student friendly, flexible, purposeful format of question papers, ensuring effective coverage of syllabi through a variety and specially worked and understandable large number of questions. Further, the evaluation method or chances affected thereto have to be communicated to the students right at the commencement of the academic session as the same is obligatory under NAAC requirements.

Transformation

Traditional approach with regard to setting of question papers does not commensurate with present day requirement and hence should be discarded with. The question papers need be so constructed as would ask questions on knowledge base, analytical understanding and skill development – all spread over to large answer (descriptive/problem solving/essay type) specifying the length of answers in words as is the practice in IGNOU, accommodate different types of tests like MCQs and SAQs. This argument is based on the fact that the examinations are now conducted fair and clean. Further, this practice would provide for a variety in syllabi coverage for a course of study. Moreover, preparation of a detailed marking scheme giving value points and key answers for the guidance of evaluators help in minimizing vagueness. Model question papers with complete marking scheme need also be constructed for the guidance of students and in absence of active involvement of teachers progress can not be achieved towards making examinations valid, reliable and powerful instruments in the qualitative improvements in teaching learning process. Further, for obtaining valid and objective scoring, there is need to lay special thrust towards evolving new modified procedures in designing and enriching question papers which would result in better changes on the instructional front and improve materials of the curriculum. Thus, aforesaid components of the curriculum management are inter-linked and any improvement in only, one component, though, will have a chain impact on the other components too. This would mean that efforts are to be made to deal effectively with the processes and procedures associated with the evaluation and focus on other issues involved would result in value-added commerce education. It is in place to state that 'continuous evaluation' component in commerce and business studies is equally indispensable and its introduction would be an important step towards the integration of teaching-learning and examinations and the same also a requirement under NAAC (Refer to Benchmark criterion 2(9). The present examination system judges the students merit on memorizing performance. The continuous evaluation neither replaces the external term end examination nor increases the frequency of examinations. Evaluation has to be a chain process and continuous evaluation thus, enables:

- To provide a student an opportunity to make his SWOT Analysis and act as a motivating force for him to engage in studies throughout the academic session.
- To provide a teacher an opportunity to employ a variety of evaluation strategies like a set of tests, quizzes, home assignments, reviews, vice voce, evaluation games, etc.

However, over the period certain developments took place in the world of business. This necessitated the review and revisiting of the commerce curriculum. Accordingly, 2-Day Workshop was organized by the Department of Commerce between October 15-16, 2008. During the process of redesigning the course contents, the designated groups were required to work within the reference frame that included:

(i) highlighting of course objectives;

(ii) sub-unitisation of course content;

(iii) pedagogy of transaction;

(iv) construction of model question papers (Shafi, *et al*, 2008).

The workshop inter alia recommended that the student mindset from traditional 'job seeking' to 'job providing' be ensured. Accordingly, attitude for entrepreneurship needs to be imbibed among students. The workshop also considered the B. Com (Professional) programme in Accounting and Marketing. However, with the passage of time B.Com (Honours) programme was also introduced and is in operation at present. The University adopted Single Paper Scheme. Sequel to it the Department again organized a workshop on 16th October, 2012 wherein two papers in each module were merged to reduce the course structure confined to four papers only. How this mechanism will benefit the academic performance of commerce students, time will decide? The aforesaid brief historical note reflects that commerce curriculum went through drastic changes from time to time – as far instance, introducing vocation programme, add-on courses, Honours programme, module pattern, single paper pattern and so on.

Resurrection

The University needs to take effective steps to renew the vital practices with regard to curriculum evaluation a discarded over the period:

- Ask the evaluators to submit a detailed report regarding the general character of answer scripts evaluated along with some suggestions for improvement.

- Ask to discuss a question paper and test checking of 10 answer scripts picked up at random when there are two or more evaluators to ensure uniformity in the scheme of marketing.
- BOUS in Commerce should conduct comprehensive analysis based on paper-wise and merit-wise and draw policy implications leading to overall improvement in the curriculum management.
- Moderation of question papers for undergraduate courses should be initiated and involvement of senior teachers in the colleges in this regard actively engaged to ensure zero defects question papers.
- The panel of paper setters and examiners appointed by BOUS in commerce based on the experience, exposure and expertise should be strictly adhered to at the operational level. It is in place to state that teaching-learning and evaluation has been accorded top priority under NAAC and ranks No. 1 among 7 bench mark criteria for assessment and accreditation of an institution in college sector.
- Students of Commerce and business studies ought not be put to any discomfort or disadvantageous position with regard to the intervening gaps during the period of examination. A member from the faculty shall be involved in the process of Date Sheet formulation.

Conclusion

To sum up, bench-marking assumes an added significance to meet the requirements of modern industry, business and society in the era of globalisation. Continuous monitoring and comparing performance against leaders anywhere in the world to identify short comings and undertake measures to improve our performance need be the objective of policy-makers on this end as well.

REFERENCES

A. Gani (1995), "Workshop on Re-orientation of Commerce Curriculum – A Report', *The Business Review*, 1(1); 103 to 105.

NAAC (2001), "Manual for Self-Study for Affiliated/Constituent Colleges, National Assessment and Accreditation Council, Bangalore: 16 to 32. 1.

Shafi, S. M. *et al.,* (2008), Re-structuring of Commerce curriculum (Workshop Proceedings), Department of Commerce, University of Kashmir.

CHAPTER

9

Higher Education
Student Value Creation through Innovative Interventions

ABSTRACT

The present paper focuses on student value creation in an educational institution. A variety of initiatives are suggested in this context. Student-centric pedagogy, continuous internal evaluation, skill development for employability, career counseling, thrust on imbibing values, etc., are a few initiatives to develop an integrated personality under a triangular framework on head, heart and hand.

Introduction

The academic behaviour of teachers in the Higher Education Institutions (HIEs) demands an immediate attention by them in creating and building upon an enriched academic environment towards a positive social change. The teachers are desired a shift in their outlook seeking professional engagements to adopt newer strategies in educational process. Organizations exist mainly for a specific purpose:

- For private sector the purpose is to enhance shareholder value.
- For public sector the main purpose is enhancing stake-holder value.

- For educational institutions the focus is on student value creation.

The Study

Rationale

The students pursuing higher education in academic colleges by and large are poor thinkers and poor communicators. They are less self-motivated and thus poor performers. The teaching-learning process sans thinking does not make any academic improvement. A teacher by his profession is creative and innovative and no people are above the level of its teachers. Every teacher has uniqueness and originality because style is individual. And he is equipped readily with an inimitable and effective style of teaching to ignite minds and to provoke young students to ponder over and develop self-confidence so as to explore intellectual horizons independently. It is in this backdrop that the present paper has been attempted to focus on student value creation in the context of higher education vision 2025.

Objectives

The present study pursues the following objectives:

1. To identify the areas of educational quality deficit.
2. To find the ways for balanced academic development.
3. To offer some recommendations for improvement.

Methodology

The study primarily is conceptual in nature and based on an analysis of available literature. However, some empirical evidences in support of certain phenomena have also been investigated.

Discussion and Analysis

The role played by educational institutions in the process of growth and persistent advancement of countries is accepted by all and sundry. Education refers to any act or experience that has a formative effect on the mind, character or physical ability of an individual. It is a process by which society through institutions transmits its cultural heritage – knowledge, values, skills – from one generation to another. A variety of strategies are to be cracked towards student value creation in higher education. The following core issues are deliberated upon threadbare in the context of Jammu and Kashmir:

- Employing student-centric pedagogy to enhance value to the teaching-learning-evaluation process.
- Strengthening internal evaluation mechanism in the era of reduced thrust on year-end external examinations.
- Accelerating IQAC functioning towards institutional performance for effective NAAC accreditation and re-accreditation.
- Blending wisdom with skill especially in social sciences in the changed employment scenario.
- Addressing ill-effects and far reaching implications of shrinking space for research in the affiliating system.
- Organizing co-curricular activities and forging public-private partnership for institutional infrastructure development.
- Introducing Hon's programmes and add-on courses at undergraduate level for gaining thorough exposure in specialised areas.
- Focusing on inclusiveness with equity to ensure fair chances and opportunities to the citizenry of the state.
- Initiating effective measures to overcome adverse impact of social decadence.
- Initiating programmes for career counseling to channelise student potential towards right direction.

Student-centric Pedagogy

The science students are exposed to practice in laboratories. It offers them an opportunity to blend theory and application of a particular phenomenon. They are totally wedded to lab work that adds to their intrinsic academic worth.

The colleges imparting instruction in social sciences attempt varied and multi-dimensional interventions. Dialogue' and' Defense' are very important methodologies as regards social sciences. The present pedagogy under the aforesaid captions is organized keeping in view a variety of preset objectives.

- To reactivate students in order to double their efforts to effectuate enthusiasm in their studies.
- To hone skills for intellectual argumentation among social science students to defend or otherwise a particular concept, theory or thought etc.
- To add value to the process of teaching-learning-evaluation by exercising zero tolerance for process risk in terms of academic loss and wastage.

The students of all the BA classes appear in 'Dialogue' and 'Defense' in batches for select units in each course of study. A team of experts from other colleges in the cluster is invited to conduct these innovative academic activities for evaluating learning outcome.

The faculty engaged in the science and art of business education has been striving hard to harness talent; sharpen skills, instill insight and promote analytical mind set among students. The concerned academics and researchers groom intellectual capital for various professions to serve the society at large. A variety of instructional strategies preferably activity oriented accordingly are used in business sciences including accounting education. The conventional methodology of course is aggressively in operation across the country.

The Case method and Brain storming mix has proven an effective teaching-learning pedagogy in accounting education. After formulating a case with regard to a firm on a particular problem by 2 or 3 students it is circulated among a bigger group (say 10 participants) for their analysis and evaluation. A Brain storming session is organized to generate creative and innovative ideas that help to find out reliable and workable solutions to the problems based on collective wisdom. Teaching-learning process performs this way a simulation tool modeled on the philosophy of leaning-by-doing. The process becomes thrilling, enjoyable, stress free and makes students enthusiastic and adventurous.

The teachers are quite familiar with the contemporary pedagogical practices but in general do not employ same while transacting course content. The UGC has widened the operational domain of the college lecturers who have been re designated as Assistant/Associate Professors. The teaching has necessarily to be supported by empirical and practice based input requiring Assistant/Associate Professors to be actively engaged in research on latest trends in their respective academic disciplines.

Internal Evaluation Mechanism

The need for reforms in examination system has always been felt. Single paper scheme system was introduced in the academic session 2010 with a twin purpose:

1. to reduce examination cycle, and
2. to relieve examinees of stress.

Thus to make more working days available for teaching-learning process. The year-end examination from the commencement till the declaration of results consumes at least a period of three months.

The affiliating universities may continue with single paper scheme. The society desires that individuals prove that they have acquired appropriate expertise and knowledge by passing through frequent and extensive evaluation. It is therefore quite essential to strengthen the continuous internal evaluation mechanism with a sincerity of purpose. The focus of teaching-learning-evaluation has to be on process enrichment and value addition to a significant extent. The whole process must result in real learning rather than mere passing of examinations and obtaining degree certificates.

Assessment and Accreditation

The IQACs wherever established of course with some exceptions are dormant, dysfunctional, and isolated. These are to be effective, empowered and alert to the developments taking place around the academic world. The IQACs shall organize frequently rigorous training programmes for the faculty and staff. Once citizens of the state are fully sensitised with regard to the provisions of the RTI Act (2009) the IQACs which are store house of institutional information and documentation could realise the essence of their role. The moments tick off fast to hold IQACs answerable so a SWOT analysis needs to be attempted as every strength offers an opportunity and every weakness a threat. The IQACs are expected to bring together all the stakeholders to work in tandem to achieve institutional goals.

Skill Based Employment

The social sciences and humanities at undergraduate level constitute around 80 per cent in terms of enrolment followed by sciences 11 per cent and business sciences 9 per cent. The changed employment scenario especially in the light of Rangarajan Committee recommendations is tilted in favour of skill development. The academic knowledge, theoretic in nature, is to be supported by extensive training in soft skills. The convergence of wisdom with skill in social sciences and humanities is quite essential.

The concerned faculty is expected to ponder over and design and develop courses of study on soft skills to achieve the objective of vocationalisation of social sciences through introducing skill oriented add-on courses. Course structure accordingly needs to be re-engineered by incorporating at least one skill oriented course along with three other traditional courses of study in each subject combination. This way the social sciences and humanities students also be able to carve due space for themselves in the job market.

Shrinking Research Space

The shrinking space for research activity in colleges has long-term ill effects and far reaching implications. The institutional research activities in terms of minor and major research projects funded by national level organizations are miserably invisible. The quantum of research output at individual faculty level in terms of publications like books, monographs, papers, articles, write ups, book reviews, case studies, etc., is gradually on decline. As a sequel to it faculty is not participating to present papers at national level seminars and conferences organized outside the state. The state goes unrepresented and the faculty deprives itself of exposure gained by participating in such academic events.

The societies that are conscious always focus on research to ignite thinking process that enables to churn out new thoughts and ideas. The need of the hour therefore is to re-energise research activities in the college sector especially in the era of globalisation and accreditation rather than to be complacent by doing away with such activities.

Social Decadence Wayout

The core of social decadence is attributed to erosion of higher human values: honesty, integrity, reverence, austerity, discipline, tolerance, courage, truth, seeking knowledge, etc. Emancipation has been a stated and cherished goal of education. Education sans close proximity between principles and practices results in erosion. There is an articulated policy and principles of universal values that has stood guarantee to human civilization through the corridors of human history. The problem is in the practices that have moved miles away from the stated principles. Educational practices now are guided by short-term goals and gains. The students are required to be embedded with higher human values to groom their overall personality.

The force behind transparency is ethics; whereas law governs disclosure. The former is a voluntary affair and the latter a mandatory one. Transparency has close proximity with or is the outcome of value education. The society needs be evolved through value education to such a level that the citizens share every piece of information willingly and voluntarily.

The concept of education primarily is the function of (knowledge, skill, values). The quality education is knowledge driven, skill oriented, and value based. It is the multiple effect rather than an additive one of the aforesaid elements. High performance in terms of quality education is the result of more and more contribution of all these elements.

The institutions that have a strategic role in the process of inculcating/teaching of values (honesty, integrity, tolerance, courage, truth, brotherhood etc.) are: home, school/college/university, peer group, media and society at large. Home occupies the bottom-line position in the pyramid of hierarchy. Teacher has a pivotal role being a friend, philosopher and guide. The role of peer group is highly acknowledged. Media has a distinction because of its spread; civil society is always at forefront in this respect.

The following experiences easily clarify how values are practiced and taught:

- That a child brought a branch of poplar tree from the back yard of the mosque located in his vicinity. When his parents saw this small branch in his hand they were shivered. Grandmother of the child immediately rushed to the kitchen and took a chopped log of wood used as fuel those days for mud stoves and threw it in the compound of the mosque to compensate. This is how values (honesty) are practiced.
- That a well learned scholar (Jenab Kalbi Sadiq) while delivering a lecture says that a prayer started by saying Allahoakber. All of a sudden somebody outside the mosque cries hai Ram mujhe bachao. On the one hand there is a good connect between Allah and His subject and on the other there is a human being in need of immediate help. What to do? Break the nimaz and rush to help the suffering. This is how values (universal brotherhood) are taught.
- The society today is in a deep crisis. There is value erosion, decay or bankruptcy. There is moral vacuum and ethical deficit. The evil in the form of greed, corruption, money mania, no respect for elders, arrogance, vulgarity, cruelty, violence and so forth has been wide spread. Different education committees and commissions constituted over the years emphasised up on inclusion of value education in curriculum. The best fit is to be established between principles and practices as well as teaching of well

established ethical standards and social code of conduct that have gained currency over years. There are two opinions: one focusing on inculcation of values by setting an example; whereas the other laying stress on its teaching. The purpose in both is to learn and thus we believe in the convergence of the two as gathered through the aforesaid experiences.

The value based education is not a onetime affair. It has a perpetuity and sustenance and is cumulative in effect because one learns from cradle to grave is an old adage. Every possible effort is to be made to overcome evil and promote virtues in the society. Therefore value education is essential to help in improving the value system in the society. The board of school education and the universities in the state have to play a gigantic role in this regard.

The democracies across the globe empower their citizens through information pertaining to every aspect of governance. The societies that are conscious and have high regard for social values are always transparent in their conduct. Right to information and value education operate in tandem and perfect combination.

The CIC in a recent seminar said that the Right to Information Act cannot become popular and strong unless it is debated and discussed by people. Thus the following steps may be initiated to popularise this tool of empowerment with due regard to value based education:

- To organize awareness programmes in educational institutions frequently.
- To arrange some slots during Orientation programmes in ASCs in the universities for teachers in higher education on the subject.
- To impress up on IMPA to conduct capsule courses on value education – right to information mix for civil services officers.
- To activate media – electronic and print to deliberate upon and publish on the subject.

- To organize Panel Discussions on the subject with due participation of civil society, academics and bureaucracy as panelists.
- To publish proceedings of the seminars/workshops in the form of booklets for wider circulation and dissemination.
- To invite citizens share their rich experiences in order to maintain an inventory of values in our social context for general awareness of people.
- To publish the Right to Information Act (2009) in all the languages spoken in the state.

The sincerity of purpose could be attained when value based education perform a driving force for right to information to create a fair society. Both need to be discussed simultaneously.

The two are different – being educated and being literate. One can have a professional degree to show against ones name but can be called literate. But being educated depends on how one conducts in different situations and behaves in the society.

The literacy is promoted and efforts are followed to gain degrees to acquire highest positions in the society. To educate is to learn the truthful and meaningful way of life with due regard to honesty, sympathy, brotherhood, kindness , humility and courage.

The day is not far off when the society will be in deep crisis of its own kind. The society in the first earnest is required to respond more effectively to the challenge educate the young generation. The challenge is huge that needs collective effort. (Jan Kounsar: 2011).

Inclusiveness and Equity

The gross enrolment ratio (GER) reflects the inclusion of the different sections of population. To include minorities or marginalised sections and women in particular in the main stream system of education. Educational institutions are established to achieve defined objectives. They are required to offer uniform pattern of education and its transaction for diverse social and cultural groups. This demands identifying elements of quality assurance in education and analyzing inter-institution variations in content and dissemination. This will prove helpful in improving equity, quality, and excellence (IOS 2011). The expansion, access and inclusion must move in line with suitability, relevance and equity.

Co-curricular Activities

The institutions of higher education in this state as elsewhere organize special functions on their annual day. The day is celebrated at the close of the academic session. It provides an opportunity to assess the achievements and shortfalls. The students are actively associated in all the segments of the programme. Rather, they manage all the activities by themselves. The presentation of annual report of college activities is a special feature of the annual day function. Felicitation and distribution of certificates of merit in due acknowledgement to the students, faculty and staff of the college for their exemplary performance in different academic pursuits forms another segment of the programme. The function generally begins with playing of college anthem (tarana) by a group of students written in Urdu, Hindi or Kashmiri. The tarana is a reflection of the vision, mission, goals and objectives of the institution. Every institution works towards realising its institutional vision. The cultural activities performed by the students exhibit their hidden talent. They need an outlet to showcase their potential and creativity. The students of today are not shy as they are exposed to the environment. However, they need mentoring and proper direction to channelise their potential. The various activities performed on the occasion include plays and skits, songs under different styles, musical performances, martial arts, game shows and so forth. The students anchor different segments of the function with a view to work independently.

The audience comprising students, faculty, staff, members of civil society, alumni, former teachers, etc., enjoy every item of the programme with a great fun. Especially students are seen highly jubilant and appreciate the performances of their fellow students by putting their hands together. The gathering on this occasion is addressed by the guests with special focus on students to work hard and smart and be confident to face the challenges of real life. To prove productive citizens to serve the society in different walks of life, the students need to acquire latest knowledge through a rigorous academic process duly embedded with value education and skill orientation in their respective disciplines. Total personality development of students is the hallmark of an effective education system; otherwise, lopsided development of personality of its citizens has made a havoc of life that the society witnesses today.

The curricular and co-curricular activities have equal significance in the teaching-learning process. Thus creation and development of infrastructure to meet adequate requirements for both is essential. Where a lecture theater, laboratory, library are essential, equally auditorium, conference hall, seminar-dialogue room are important. The educational planners are desired to focus their attention towards these requirements. The role of private participation in higher education can hardly be undermined. Private sector has aggressively been participating in teacher education programmes. The active participation of private players is desired now in other branches of knowledge as well. The setting up of advanced institutions in higher education sector by private organizations is quite essential in this regard for creating physical infrastructure. The government sector with mass expansion to ensure accessibility is not in a position to shoulder heavy financial burden on the development of basic infrastructural requirements. Under new mechanism government may meet recurring costs in respect of staff salaries. Further, the government is now shifting to accrual accounting system and it will be easy to invite private players for participation in equity. The government sector may withdraw and divest from the age old institutions and focus on newly established institutions at far off peripheries in the state. Of course, public-private partnership in higher education can offer sound solutions to many problems currently confronted with.

Career Counselling

The full fledged process involved in planning a career contains all aspects of students personality. The job of a professional is to help a student find his/her career. But in Kashmir neither counseling culture nor career counselors are available in schools and colleges to guide the students. Conversely in developed countries counselors play an important role in grooming the career of students.

The following four stages are involved in choosing a career:

- *First stage* of career choice is self-awareness. This involves looking at skills, values, interests, and personality of a student. Thus attempting a SWOT analysis to analyse strengths and weaknesses as well as opportunities and threats.
- *Second stage* is to gather information on the opport-unities open with regard to the courses and careers available in or outside the country. And among those opportunities which course and career suit a respective personality.
- *Third stage* is making decisions and friends, family, career counselors and tutors all play an important role in this regard. It is the stage where student in consultation with others decide what career to choose keeping in view the information gathered as above. The decision involves more of student participation.
- *Fourth stage* relates to action or implementation and student has to work hard for his/her career. At this stage students should set for them the ultimate goal. Meanwhile students can make short-term goals with regard to timeline as well to ascertain whether they are following the right track.

Conclusions

The process value addition is closely associated with the academic performance indicators of the faculty. Once students divorce readymade note culture and rote memorisation and make nights of the faculty sleepless to find out answers to their non-routine and unknown queries the objective of Student Value Creation is achieved. The present paper finally sums up the higher education-vision 2025 based on aforesaid discussion as under:

1. To shift from teaching to managing student real learning appears mandatory.
2. To make student a good performer, imaginative and innovative in his outlook.
3. To switch over to score card from marks sheet.
4. To focus on 5 critical non-cognitive skills: knowledge and creativity; team work and group spirit; resilience and reformation; planning and organization; ethics and integrity.
5. To create and develop infrastructure to meet curricular and co-curricular activities. Public-private partnership in higher education can offer sound solutions to many problems currently confronted with.

REFERENCES

Jan Kounser (2011), Fast but False, G. K., 24, No. 297, p. 9.

CHAPTER

Higher Education

Zero Tolerance for Process Risk

ABSTRACT

The higher education institutions primarily lack punch. There is low value addition and high process risk. The present paper on the one hand focuses on competitive environment and exemplary work culture with total social commitment in the teaching-learning process and on the other hand examination and evaluation reforms. Nothing can improve unless there is zero tolerance for process risk. Performance audit of all the stakeholders is thus a must. The discussion on this paper is appended under Annexure-1. ???

Introduction

The second criteria under NAAC accreditation is captioned 'Teaching Learning-Evaluation' (TLE). It carries 450 score points or 45 per cent of the total weightage. And spreads over six key aspects and thirty core activities. This criterion is pivotal as regards process effectiveness leading to excellence. "Excellence is always result of good intentions, sincere efforts, intelligent direction and sincere execution" (NAAC, 2004) All this demands an exemplary work culture with a social commitment in a competitive environment.

The Framework

Problems

The following media highlights are quite disturbing. These reflect the contemporary state of health of higher education sector.

- 10,000 including Ph.Ds and MBAs apply against 120 posts of chowkidars in Delhi Government (The Hindu).
- 6000 apply for 26 posts graduates and PGs jostle for class IV Jobs (Greater Kashmir).

Objectives

The present paper in the aforesaid back drop has been attempted in pursuance of the following objectives:

- To study the state of the process value addition in higher education sector.
- To explore ways to overcome process risk leading to excellence in higher education institutions.

Methodology

The discussion held in the perspective of Jammu and Kashmir state is based on certain arguments. An oppionnaire, a Competitive environment, work culture and social commitment four statements under each item, was administrated to 39 participants to obtain their responses. The paper, in respect of various issues, attempts to generate a debate and discussion to arrive at some conclusions and remedial measures for implementation.

Discussion

(i) Fundamental Contentions

The debate and deliberations move around a variety of arguments and counter arguments in the context of aforesaid identified problems.

- That miss-match between demand and supply in the job market appears a sound factor responsible for this state of affairs. This argument could have been further Substantiated but there has not been excellence performance achievement at institutional and individual level of students. As is clear thus:

(a) That at institutional level, 25 higher education institutions (Colleges) stand accredited by NAAC so far. Two institutions only got 'A' grade. An accredited institution, obtained 2.62 on a four point scale. People were complacent with getting 'B' grade under new scheme. But, what about the process risk to the tune of 0.58 points or 14.5 per cent at 80 per cent optimal level of performance. The public funds, spent around 200 lakhs for a period of 5 years are not justified because of under performance. A matter of serious concern! The stakeholder needs to pause and ponder over.

(b) That at individual level percentage marks (mean score) obtained by the students was 49-73 (2009). Std., deviation 4.83 and co-efficient of variance 9.70. The students, felt satisfied even at this level of low performance. The intrinsic value could have even been lower. There was a process risk of around 30.27 again at 80 per cent optimal level or performance. It reflects an inadequate value added process. The under-utilisation of public funds should have rendered all the stakeholders restless to correct this state of affairs.

- That higher education is open for all and sundry. The proper channelization after 10+2; level is missing. Students having zero aptitude for higher education should have been channelized towards acquiring hard skills. Industrial Training Institutions (ITIS) and polytechnic Colleges should welcome them. However, a stark reality is that the gross enrolment ratio (GER) at 5 per cent in Jammu and Kashmir state is the lowest. The national average at 13.48 (2007) was expected to rise to the level of 20 by the year 2015. The requisite number of the students in the relevant age group is not attracted towards higher education.
- That expansion is responsible for quality deterioration. True it may me but Jammu and Kashmir state accounts

for only 0.48 as against 1.00 in the total number of colleges for general education in the country. Keeping in view the population size of the state and the number of colleges at the national level, Jammu and Kashmir state needs 54 more colleges for general education to maintain the current national average.

The afore grim phenomenon or academic recession out rightly attributed to either:

1. Market forces, or
2. Improper channelization, or
3. Mass expansions are not well founded arguments. The fault lies somewhere else. This needs a thorough introspection at the level of all stakeholders. The education institutions are expected perpetual value additions of students under the paradigm of value chain analysis. Quality improvement in TLE' process is essential. But, it is found that the magnitude of the process risk in the system is substantially high.

Punch Lacking

The following issues are very pertinent in this regard;

- That teaching-learning-evaluation process has not attained the primary three dimensional objectives to make learners:
  (i) independent;
  (ii) interdependent; and
  (iii) confident.
- That transition of higher education from 'elite class' to 'mass-based' mechanism resulted in harmonisation of higher education with livelihood. The higher education as such cannot be divorced from employability rather has to be weded with it.
- That the LPG wave brought with it a Competitive environment. Sequel to it there has been a total shift from bottom-up to top-down approach. As says a scholar whenever any results are declared everybody concentrates on the toppers. Nobody bothers about the performance

of average students. They are in majority. Addressing their problems is need of the hour that would provide a solution to the questions confronting our education system (GK Reflection 17.02.201.). This again is a glaring example of high process risk.

- That the state of work culture is highly dismal and deplorable and sans social commitment at all levels. The ABC analysis of students registered in all the conventional faculties in the college sector in the state may reveal as under box (a).

Box (A)			
'A'	Real learners	10%	Top-line
'B'		20%	
'C'	Just Registered	70%	Bottom-line

The students falling under 'A' category are real learners. They shine not only in the state but outside as well in every walk of life. They constitute the top-line, whereas, 70 per cent students fall in the 'C' category who get themselves registered with a view to getting a certificate. They may resort to unfair practices in the examinations and create problems here and there. They contribute towards process risk to the maximum extent. The University even negates their degree certificates when it conducts entrance test for advanced studies. They need to be motivated and their processing needs additional efforts by the faculty.

The other day a Chartered Accountant friend was asked as how they create a differentiation when course of study for both of our programmes (B. Com/ M. Com or CA) are almost uniform. His reply was interesting and logically convincing as well and reproduced here under box (b).

The general academic institutions chum out graduates fit for drudgery and the lowest rate jobs (of course with some exceptions). There is simply transformation of data and information that too-obsolete.

Box (B)

You believe in short-cuts; guess work, irrelevant and obsolete study notes made available at Tuition Shops. You exercise Trick No. 1 and Trick No. 2 and so forth. You attempt 2 problems; whereas, we attempt 200 on the same topic. We are methodical and study regularly, rigorously and religiously. We comparatively put in 100 times-more labour, effort and time. Naturally we add value to the process and enjoy a cutting edge and have a comparative advantage.

It sans dissemination of Knowledge leading to wisdom and – finally; to; arrive at the truth. The system moves around low value added process; All the stakeholders contribute and are equally responsible for the high process risk.

(ii) Teaching-Learning Efficacy

The triangular paradigm of Competitive environment, work culture and social commitment is discussed and analysed in Table 10.1.

Table 10.1: Triangular Paradigm

Competitive Environment			Work Culture			Social Commitment		
Statement	+ve Response		Statement	+ve Response		Statement	+ve Response	
	No	%		No	%		Na	%
X1	35	89.75	Y1	37	94.85	Z1	36,	92.30
X2	33	84.60	Y2	34	87.20	Z2	34	87.20
X3	33	84.60	Y	33	84.60	Z3	35	89.75
X4	34	87.20	Y4	31	79.50	Z4	30	76.90
Mean		86.55			86.55			86.55

Source: Field Survey.

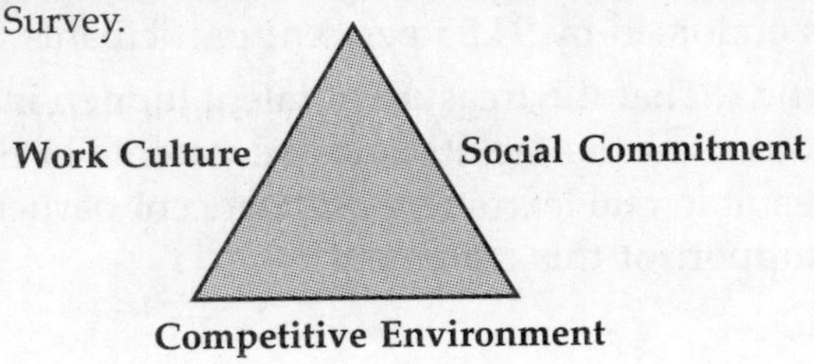

Work Culture **Social Commitment**

Competitive Environment

Competitive Environment

The higher education institutions operating in a Competitive environment need to realise:

Statement XI: That quality in the ultimate analysis is the outcome of competition and minimisation of process risk. It can be attained not only by meeting bench-marks but by beating benchmarks as well. 89.75 of the participants subscribed to this view point.

Statement X2: That the students should get an exemplary exposure, equal opportunity to put in every effort towards total preparedness for facing the real life challenges. 84.60 per cent participants held this point of view.

Statement X3: That the curriculum under competitive environment is regularly revisited, reviewed and revised in order to shape it in line with the global standards. This statement was agreed upon by 84.60 per cent participants.

Statement X4: That added focus need be on the student. Centric pedagogy and faculty accordingly have to equip with the new instructional strategies in order to improve upon quality and add value to the process. This statement was supported by 87.20 per cent participants.

Work Culture

The need of the time is to re-evaluate the approach enabling challenges of Competitive environment are to be converted into opportunities by way of an effective work culture. There fore, it is required:

Statement; Y1: That the students not only work hard but study smart with a positive attitude to create a differentiation by adding credibility to and making TLE a challenging experience reducing thereby process-risk. This statement was endorsed by 94.85 per cent participants.

Statement Y2: That the treasure of talent hidden in students is groomed by the faculty and the parents of the students to result in real learning. 87.20 per cent participants were in support of this statement.

Statement Y3: That the institution pursue flexible time-table exposing students to all the three segments of education-intellectual, emotional and spiritual for overall development of mind, body and spirit to stimulate total absorption of students in their holistic personality development. 84.60 per cent participants were in favour of this statement.

Statement Y4: That the short-cuts, guess work, mugging up etc., are replaced forth with by igniting minds for thinking, critical appraisal, creativity and innovation. This statement was appreciated by 79.50 per cent participation.

Social Commitment

The whole focus of all the stake holders necessarily has to be embedded with 'social commitment' which in turn demands:

Statement Z1: That the faculty be totally engaged in professional development and involved in exploring cotemporary advancements made in their respective fields of specialisation. This statement obtained acceptance of 92.30 per cent participants.

Statement Z2: That organizing personality and attitudinal programmes has to be mandatory' with a view to churning out world class students confident in attitude and independent' in decision-making to effect a positive social change. This statement received approval of 87.20 per cent participants.

Statement Z3: That the performance of the institutional leadership is Judged as to what extent they have been able to process available scarce resources into optimal level of value addition for social benefit. 76.90 per cent participants were in favour of this statement.

Statement Z4: That all the stake holders are expected to contribute towards the improvement in the quality of TLE with full Social Commitment. This was agreed Upon by 89.75 per cent participants.

(iii) Examination and Evaluation Reforms

The following steps need to be initiated towards reforming examination and evaluation system.

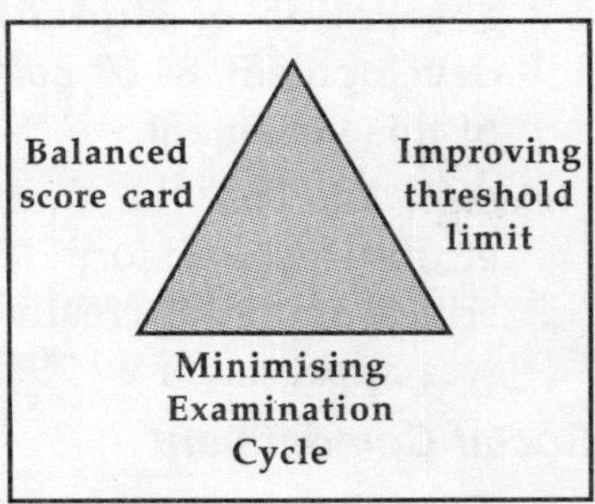

- The present very wide examination and evaluation cycle entails 2-3 months. That results in shrinkage in the days available for teaching-learning process. The following steps need to be considered for implementation in order to effect a reduction in the examination cycle:
  1. To start continuous evaluation mechanism round the academic session and keep the students fully engrossed in their studies.
  2. To implement single paper scheme of examination and relieve students of examination stress and strain. This way the regular academic transaction would start from March 1 on re-opening of the college after winter vacations. It would help in gaining more days for teaching-learning. The institutions would be abuzz of academic dispensation from March 1st to Oct 31st (8 months). From Nov 1st - 15th December examinations would be conducted and results to be out by the 10th Feb for all the degree classes.
- The present threshold limit for qualifying examination (36 or 40) is now age old and need reconsideration. It provides scope for very high process risk (44% or 40%) at 80 optimal level which is not acceptable under any educational standards especially in the era of quality education. The present threshold limit may be raised upto 45 or 50 and further an incremental basis over the period. The 'push factor effect' would make the students Work further. There also need some riders for qualifying both internal and external examinations.

- The present system of education is examination oriented. To reduce the dominance of examination the conventional 'marks card' is required to be replaced by the 'balanced score card' to reflect performance of students in all spheres of learning. The main objective is to focus on the real learning, intrinsic academic worth and overall personality development of students. Thus to accommodate scholastic as well as non-scholastic activities to form different components of the 'Balanced score card'.

Conclusions

The stake holders need to pursue a high intent. The institutional leadership, Department of higher Education and affiliating Universities are desired to provide intelligent direction. The parents and faculty render skilful execution of activities. Continuous parental support and strong backing by the faculty would provide a golden opportunity to students to move ahead fast in their academic pursuits. The students as primary stakeholders are expected to put in sincere efforts in their studies. All these put together with academic zeal and zest and total social commitment would add value to the process finally to result in excellence. All the stakeholders should be subjected to the strict social audit to encompass five cardinal components:

1. Audit of policy.
2. Audit of institution.
3. Audit of governance.
4. Audit of faculty.
5. Audit of students.

ANNEXURE-I

Discussion

Dr. Farooq A. Shah

In the contemporary knowledge era, educational excellence has become a buzz word even if experts have had considerable difficulty in evolving a concern on what the term, 'Educational Excellence' precisely stands for, yet most of these experts acknowledge that the concept is the central theme of any educational intervention effort. Given the fact the educational excellence is a relative term, it can be defined as "the degree to which the system and institutions of education are effective in providing the socio-economically viable citizens to the contemporary society".

The concept of holistic efficiency in the education system emphasises that educational excellence is the composite function of all the internal and external systemic constituent. As a matter of fact, the value addition process or teaching-learning-evaluation dynamics lies at the core of the excellence of the education system. In other words, any, compromise on the effective execution of teaching-learning-evaluation is bound to impact the efficiency of the educational system as a whole. It is in realisation of the significance of this core constituent that the National Assessment and Accreditation Council (NAAC) have assigned a weightage of 45 to the criterion of 'teaching-learning-evaluation' on assessing the excellence of affiliated and constituent colleges.

The paper under discussion "Qualitative improvement in Higher Education Institutions-Goal of Zero Tolerance for Process Risk" by Dr. Nazir Ahmad Gilkar is a right pick, laid on a well thought out framework. Building on the backdrop of the higher education scenario in Jammu and Kashmir, the author has, touched upon few characteristics of the dismal standing of the state's higher education sector. The empirical study focuses on the core constituent of the system-*viz.*: teaching, learning and evaluation. In an attempt to explore the risk associated with the-dynamic process of teaching-learning-evaluation, the paper takes up three delicate elements critical to the effectiveness of the core constituent. These include competitive environment, work culture and social commitment. The author has attempted to investigate the critical areas of the three typical dimensions and delved deep into the, factors that determine the efficacy of the teaching-learning-evaluation process.

Highlighting their role on minimising the process risk, the plethora of factors identified by the author cover all the areas on the relevant paradigms of the student, the teacher and the value addition process. Besides, the paper envisages the examination and evaluation reforms and elaborates on its three distinct areas.

By writing a paper on such a key area, the author has amply demonstrated his deep understanding of the dynamics of the quality and excellence of the higher, education institutions and the system as a whole. The paper has opened up new vistas for studying the tacit but equally crucial elements of the educational excellence.

Dr. Farooq Ahmad Shah is Nodal officer, Government Degree College, Sumbal, Kashmir.

CHAPTER

Higher Education
Implementation of Performance Budgeting

ABSTRACT

The present study attempts to correlate physical performance with financial performance in respect of HEIs – contrary to conventional budgeting, performance budgeting focuses on the purpose and traces every rupee spent with end-results in terms of physical achievements. The study is carried in the light of NAAC seven criteria to see as to why funds have not been utilised effectively because of under performance in physical units. The objective is to fix responsibility for wastage of funds and the release of funds simply based on physical performance vis-à-vis target set.

Introduction

The eminent management thinker of our times Peter Drucker has rightly pointed out, "the centre of a modern society, economy and community is not technology. It is not information. It is not productivity. It is the managed institution as the organ of society to produce results". Under this paradigm the management of an institution should re-orient its role and practice. Drucker emphasised the purpose of institutional management in the following terminology:

> *"Management exists for the sake of institution's results, it has to start with intended results and has to organize the resources of the institution to attain the results. It is the organ to make institution, whether business, church, university, hospital etc. capable of producing results".*
>
> **— (Chakraborty)**

The higher education institutions put in efforts to develop students in their:

(a) Intellectual growth, wisdom head.

(b) Change in behaviour, virtues heart.

(c) Skill development employability hand.

The objective is to make students responsible citizens to serve the society in different walls of life. Thus there is a clear distinction between the curriculum for the faculty and that one pursued by the students. The curriculum of the students is only a component of the curriculum assigned to the faculty.

The faculty is engaged in curriculum management:

(a) Conceptualisation and designing of new and revising the existing programmes and courses of study.

(b) Regular transaction in class room setting and evaluation of student achievement.

(c) They are also busy in activities like:

- *(i)* Research.
- *(ii)* Publication.
- *(iii)* Consultancy.
- *(iv)* Counseling.
- *(v)* Participation in seminars.
- *(vi)* Organizing debates and discussions.
- *(vii)* Corporate life of the institution-institutional governance through committee participation.
- *(viii)* Extension activities by bringing together the campus and the community.

The quality dimension has gained primacy in higher education sector. Efforts for sustenance and enhancement of quality in higher education institutions (HEIs) got impetus with the establishment of National Assessment and Accreditation Council (NAAC) in the year 1994. The performance achievements of HEIs and in turn of the faculty has been assessed through an inbuilt mechanism based on 07 key result areas comprising 36 crore activities integrated on 1000 score points.

Conventional Budgeting

The conventional budgeting concentrates more on controlling actual expenditure with reference to the budgeted expenditure. It lays emphasis only on the amount of expenditure to be incurred. The expenditure is categorised by the 'type' of amount heads which is to be spent (*viz.:* salaries, travel expenses, printing, etc.). It contains broad heads of expenditure know as 'line items classification'. The financial outlay is not related to the physical performance visualised and achievements made or proposed to be made. Thus, conventional budgeting lacks in the 'purpose' for which money is to be spent. Following are the two weak areas, the conventional budgeting suffers from.

(i) Failure to relate costs to educational impact (accomplishments).

(ii) Separation of estimating from policy-making.

The present study in the backdrop of aforesaid discussion has been attempted in pursuance of the following objectives:

- To study the conceptual foundation of performance budgeting.
- To assess implementation of performance budgeting in higher education sector.
- To ascertain response of different stakeholders towards performance budgeting.

The methodology adopted to attain the preset objectives includes:

(i) The literature available on the subject in the form of books, journals, magazines and that available on the websites has been gathered and re-arranged for conceptual analysis.

(ii) The conventional budget dawn in respect of a particular institution has been studied and the budgeted expenditure apportioned to the key result areas (NAAC performance criteria) based on their respective weights. It was followed by assigning the said expenditure to the actual performance achieved. On completion of the academic session actual accomplishments have been compared with the budgets, variances ascertained and investigated. The amount of funds wasted owing to under performance criterion-wise has been worked out for which response has to be fixed. The budgeted expenditure has finally been absorbed in the number of performance units for inner and intra institutional comparison.

(iii) The response of stakeholders about the implementation of performance budgeting in HEIs has also been attempted. Discussions with college Principals were held during different academic programmes with a view to gather empirical evidence. Thus, to ascertain response a questionnaire was administered to 35 college principals. A group of 25 respondents (71.432%) cooperated and returned the same after doing the needful. Twenty statements have been classified under five groups. The data thus gathered on 5 point likert scale from highest (5) to the lowest (1) importance of each variable. The assigned scores on these scales from 5 to 1 respectively have been subject to statistical analysis. Average weighted Score (AWS) and mean in per cent has been computed. The data analsed has been presented in tabular format and interpreted subsequently.

Performance Budgeting

The concept of performance budgeting has its origin in the USA after the 2nd world war (1939-44). The term performance budgeting was first used by Hoover Commission in the USA in 1949. The application of this concept was further emphasised in the second Hoover Commission Report in 1955 (Oswal and Agarwal, 1982). The Administrative Reforms Commission of India recommended in 1967, the introduction of performance budgeting in major spending departments in India (Jain, *et al.*, 2002). The performance budgeting thus has ushered a new era in Government budgeting which provides for appraisal for performance as well as follow-up measures.

The practice followed prior to the advent of performance budgeting, budget in the Government was prepared on the basis of financial account heads. Now budgets are sought to be made performance-wise also. This helps in planning more realistically. Further, the expenditure is to be related to physical targets. In short for proper planning and effective control, performance budgeting is very important.

The success or otherwise of the performance budgeting would depend on the following pre-requisites:

- The expenditure should result in certain activities.
- The output of the activities should be measurable.
- The cost per unit should be estimated, ascertained and compared for improved performance.
- The standards should neither be too strict not too liberal.
- The standards used for budgeting should be attainable by an efficient performance.
- The information and reporting should gear up to cover both financial and physical performance details.
- The faculty should be involved in the preparation of budget and evaluation as human factor could not be ignored.

The performance budgeting focuses on end result. Thus, under performance budgeting emphasis has shifted from the means of accomplishments to accomplishment itself. A real performance budgeting gives a meaningful indication of how rupees are expected to turn into results. Functions, programmes and activities form the framework within which performance budgeting is prepared and administered, departments like education, health, social forestry, etc., can be separate functions in the government sector. Under each function there are different programmes and activities and physical achievements of targets are assessed.

The programmes and activities in respect of a function like education can be studied under two areas as regards their scope, *viz.*:

(i) macro level; and

(ii) micro level.

At the former stage, it could be number of colleges and universities to be set up and established etc. However, the later situation is an assessment of HEIS-colleges and universities could be made in terms of activities accomplishment as is done in the present study.

The Box (a) gives highlights of the comparative salient features of performance budgeting and traditional budgeting:

Box (a)

Performance Budgeting vis-a-Traditional Budgeting

Performance Budgeting	Traditional Budgeting
• Flow of decision is upward	• Flow of decision is downward
• Follows the function-programme-activity classification	• Classification of expenses is by object
• Approach is prospective	• Approach of retrospective

Source: Constructed from the literature gathered from Cost Accounting (2002) by Jain, Narang and Dhingra.

The performance budgeting is thus a formal system applied for establishing:

- The objectives of an institution.
- The activities contributing towards realising objectives.
- The inputs devoted to these activities.
- The achievements attained.

Exploratory Study

The budgeted expenditure for a particular year in respect of a college has been Rs. 276.65 lakhs. The faculty and Staff salaries accounted for 91.60 of the total budgeted expenditure.

The budgeted expenditure for different heads of accounts like salaries, travel expenditure etc., constitutes input costs.

Performance budgeting as a control tool serves to result in the effective utilisation of resources and proper monitoring of the activities carried out. For this purpose both physical performances achieved and quantum of financial expenditure made are monitored. Thus, an inventory of activities – key results areas – NAAC criteria in the present context forms targets. Budgeted expenditure (input costs) are apportioned to each activity based on its respective weightage followed by absorption in performance units. The highest accomplishments enable an institution to effect cost efficiency.

The NAAC assessment takes care of the following seven key result areas:

(i) Curricular Aspects (50/5).
(ii) Teaching-Learning and Evaluation (450/45).
(iii) Research Consultancy and Extension (100/10).
(iv) Infrastructure and Learning Process (100/10).
(v) Student Support and Progression (100/10).
(vi) Governance and Leadership (150/15).
(vii) Innovative practices (50/5).

The key result area *(iv)* is of more input nature than that of output. The analysis reveals as under:

Table 11.1: Curricular Aspects

Core Activities	Weightage		Budgeted Expenditure (Rs. in lakhs)
	Scores	%Age	
Curricular Design and Development	10	1.0	2.77
Academic Flexibility	15	1.5	4.15
Feed back on curriculum	10	1.0	2.77
Curricular update	05	0.5	1.39
Best practices in curricular aspect	10	1.0	2.77
Total	**50**	**5.0**	**13.85**

The curricular aspect criterion is spread over 5 crore activities carrying 50 score points constituting 5 per cent of the performance index. The total budgeted expenditure envisaged to this performance area has been Rs. 13.85 lakhs (Table 11.1).

Table 11.2: Teaching-Learning and Evaluation

Core Activities	Weightage		Budgeted Expenditure (Rs. in lakhs)
	Scores	%Age	
Admission process and student profile	30	3.0	8.30
Catering to diverse needs	45	4.5	12.45
Teaching-Learning process	270	27.0	74.69
Teacher Quality	65	6.5	17.98
Evaluation Process and Reforms	30	3.0	8.30
Best practices	10	1.0	2.77
Total	**450**	**45.00**	**124.49**

The teaching-learning and evaluation is a very significant key performance area as it carries 450 score points or 45 per cent of the aggregate key performance index. This key performance area is spread over 6 core activities and the budgeted expenditure earmarked for this key result area has been Rs. 124.49 lakhs (Table 11.2).

Table 11.3: Research Consultancy and Extension

Core Activities	Weightage		Budgeted Expenditure (Rs. in lakhs)
	Scores	%Age	
Promotion of Research	15	1.5	4.15
Research and Publication output	25	2.5	6.91
Consultancy	05	0.5	1.38
Extension Activities	40	4.0	11.06
Collaborations	05	0.5	1.39
Best practices in research, consultancy and extension	10	1.0	2.77
Total	**100**	**10.0**	**27.66**

The research, consultancy and extension criterion covers 6 core activities having 100 score points or 10 per cent of the total key performance index. The budgeted expenditure earmarked for this result area amounts to Rs. 27.66 lakhs (Table 11.3).

Table 11.4: Infrastructure and Learning Resource

Core Activities	Weightage		Budgeted Expenditure (Rs. in lakhs)
	Scores	%Age	
Physical facilities for learning	20	2.0	5.53
Maintenance of infrastructure	10	1.0	2.77
Library as a learning resource	35	3.5	9.68
ICT as learning resource	15	1.5	4.15
Other facilities	10	1.0	2.77
Best practices in development of infrastructure and library resource	10	1.0	2.77
Total	**100**	**10.0**	**27.67**

The infrastructure and learning resource criterion is spread over 6 crore activities. The total score points attributed to this key result area are 100 forming 10 per cent of the aggregate key performance index. Whereas budgeted expenditure has been earmarked Rs. 27.67 lakhs (Table 11.4).

Table 11.5: Student Support and Progression

Core Activities	Weightage		Budgeted Expenditure (Rs. in lakhs)
	Scores	%Age	
Student progression	30	3.0	8.30
Student Support	30	3.0	8.30
Student Activities	30	3.0	8.30
Best practices in Student Support in progression	10	1.0	2.77
Total	**100**	**10.0**	**27.67**

The student support and progression has been earmarked Rs. 27.67 lakhs for the four criteria with score points 100 constituting 10 per cent of the aggregate.

Table 11.6: Governance and Leadership

Core Activities	Weightage		Budgeted Expenditure (Rs. in lakhs)
	Scores	%Age	
Institutional vision and leadership	15	1.5	4.15
Organizational Arrangements	20	2.0	5.53
Strategy development and deployment	30	3.0	8.30
Human Resource Management	40	4.0	11.06
Financial Management and Resource Mobilisation	35	3.5	9.68
Best practices in Governance and Leadership	10	1.0	2.76
Total	**100**	**15.0**	**41.48**

The governance and leadership covers 6 core activities entailing 150 score points or constituting 15 per cent of the aggregate key performance index. Rs. 41.48 lakhs of the annual budgeted expenditure has been earmarked towards this result area (Table 11.6).

Table 11.7: Innovative Practice

Core Activities	Weightage		Budgeted Expenditure (Rs. in lakhs)
	Scores	%Age	
Internal quality assurance system	20	2.0	5.53
Inclusive Practices	15	1.5	4.15
Stakeholders Relationship	15	1.5	4.15
Total	**50**	**5.0**	**13.83**

The innovative practices covers 3 core activities having 50 scoe points or 5 per cent of the total key performance index. An amount of Rs. 13.83 lakhs has been envisaged for this key performance as given in (Table 11.7).

Table 11.8: Performance Budgeting – Key Performance Area-wise Analysis (Rs. in lakhs)

Key Physical Area	Weightage		Budgeted Expenditure (Rs. in lakhs)	Achievements		Wastage Responsibility Fixing
	Score	%age		Physical	Financial (Rs. in lakhs)	
Curricular Aspects	50	5.0	13.85	40 (4)	11.08	2.77
Teaching learning and evaluation	450	45.0	124.49	360 (36)	99.59	24.90
Research Consultancy	100	10.0	27.66	80 (8)	22.13	5.53
Infrastructure and Learning Evaluation	100	10.0	27.67	80 (8)	22.14	5.53
Student Support and Progression	100	10.0	27.67	80 (8)	22.14	5.53
Governance and Leadership	150	15.0	41.48	120 (12)	33.18	8.30
Innovative Practices	50	5.0	13.83	40 (4)	11.06	2.77
Total	**1000**	**100.0**	**276.65**	**800 (80)**	**221.32**	**55.33**

The budgeted expenditure at 80 per cent level of performance accomplishment or end-result achieved in the present context could be justified to the tune of Rs. 221.32 lakhs, whereas, an amount of Rs. 55.33 lakhs at this level of performance achievement stands wasted in the sample college during the year of study. Thus, responsibility has to be fixed for the wastage of funds because of under performance (Table 11.8).

The budgeted expenditure has finally been absorbed in different budget units. The analysis has been attempted with a view to make inter institution performance comparison possible within each group of institutions to work as a control mechanism. The comparative analysis has been done in respect of expectations and achievements at 80 per cent with regard to the annual budgeted expenditure in terms of a variety of parameters *viz.:*

Table 11.9: Performance Budgeting: Unit-wise Analysis

Curricular Aspects	Annual Budgeted Expenditure (Rs. in lakhs)	Expectations		Achievement (80%)	
		Unit (No.)	Cost/ Unit Rs.	Unit/ (No)	Cost/ Unit Rs.
Cost per teaching working day	276.65	180	153694	144	192118
Cost per teacher working day	276.65	9000	3074	7200	3842
Cost per teaching working hour	276.65	1080	25616	864	32019
Cost per teacher working hour	276.65	54000	512	43200	640
Cost per student	276.65	2000	13833	1600	17291
Cost per equivalent student	276.65	2000	13833	1680	16467

(i) Cost per teaching working day.
(ii) Cost per teacher working day.
(iii) Cost per teaching working hour.
(iv) Cost per teacher working hour.
(v) Cost per student.
(vi) Cost per equivalent student.

Empirical Evidence

The response gathered from the Principals with regard to the implementation of performance budgeting in the college sector has been analysed and the aggregate analysis is given in the Table 11.10.

The information ascertained on 5 dimensions reveals that:
(i) Conceptual Exposition.
(ii) Motivational Drive.
(iii) Institutional up-gradation.

(iv) Control mechanism have got mean score more than 60 per cent indicating thereby that the participants are interested in the implementation of performance budgeting, by organizing sensitization programmes at different levels, the interest in performance budgeting would further increase as is evident by this dimension that has got mean score of 88 per cent (Table 11.10).

Table 11.10: Aggregate Analysis

Dimensions	TWS	AWS	Mean (in %age)
Conceptual Exposition	300.00	12.00	60.00
Motivational Drive	310.00	12.40	62.00
Institutional up-gradation	305.00	12.20	63.00
Control Mechanism	307.00	12.28	61.40
Sensitisation Programmes	440.00	17.60	88.00

Conclusions and Suggestions

The performance budgeting is attributed to the normal budgetary process. The estimated expenditure is presented Programmes and performance units under each programme. The expenditure is also related to the expected targets or each unit of activity at all levels of operations. Thus, periodic performance reports would be compiled by every institution and inter-institution companions could be made. Performance achievement per rupee of budgeted expenditure is the beauty of performance budgeting.

The performance budgeting would lead to work smart, innovative and competitive on the part of all stakeholders. The institutional vision, mission, goals and objectives would be translated into reality.

The need of the hour is to change mindset at each level with a view to make efforts for implementation of performance budgeting the sensitisation of all concerned with regard to performance budgeting in higher education sector is urgently required. In this regard the following steps need be initiated;

- That IQAC at each college level should organize workshops to develop, contextual understanding and prepare stakeholders to perform accordingly.
- That UGC Academic Staff College should also conduct some sessions using orientation programmes and refresher courses on this vital theme.
- That the NAAC should initiate the process of developing and disseminating the relevant material on the subject so that the stakeholders have a conceptual exposition.
- That the conduct of special studies on the theme of performance budgeting should be encouraged and findings shared with the faculty so that performance budgeting is used as a mechanism towards quality enhancement in the higher education sector.
- The College Principals have shown keen interest in performance budgeting as a monitoring tool of performance at institutional level. This is the mechanism for improving performance at the individual faculty level as well. Accordingly, teachers would he in a position to evaluate their performance periodically. It is also suggested that as the corporate life of the college sector in the state is governed through the committee formation, so these committees need be reclassified and made subordinate to the NAAC seven key performance areas in order to result in effective performance of the HEIs.
- That the NAAC may also consider to focus on performance budgeting as an essential component during the course of its assessment and accreditation of the HEIs.

The present study further foresees the following challenges ahead (Gilkar, 2008):

(a) That the moment tax payers become aware, they will seek information under RTT Act with regard to physical performance achieved and funds wasted as a sequel to under performance.

(b) That NAAC grading is a reflection of student value added as well. The higher institutional grading would be the reflection of student value addition and vice-versa.

(c) That responsibility has to be fixed with regard to wastage of public money consequent upon under achievement.

REFERENCES

Agarwal V. and Bhatnagar RP. (2004), Educational Administration: Supervision, Planning and Financing, Surva Publishing, Meerut.

Chakraborly. R.K. (2006), "Cost Control to Result Control – The New Business Challenge for the 21st' Century", *The Chartered Accountant*. 55(03). 427-432.

Garg. V.P. (2006), "Budget Formulation for Educational Planning, Economic versus Financial Approach", NIEPA Bulletin NIEPA, 7 (1 and 2), 42.

Gilkar. NA (2008), "Performance Budgeting in Higher Education Institutions", in Financial Sector of India (edit) by Dr. R. K. Uppal. New Century Publications, New Delhi 50-59.

Gupta, S. K. and Sharma, R. K. (2007), "Management Accounting", Kalyani Publishers, New Delhi.

ICFA University (2006), Management Accounting.

Jain, S. P., Narang KL, Dhingra, TR (2002), Cost Accounting: Principles and Practice, Kalyana Publishers Ludhiana.

John Mercer (2004), "Performance Based Budgeting".

Mohan V. K. M. (2008), "Building a Resultocracy", *The Business Line,* August 11-12.

Oswal, ML and Agarwal, RI (1982), "Performance Budgeting", *The Management Accountant*, 17 (4) 203-206.

Pancrar, U. (2005), "Performance Budgeting for Government Operations".

Shukia, PD (1983), "Administration of Education in India", Vikas Publishing House Pvt. Ltd., New Delhi.

CHAPTER

12

Higher Education
Possibility Thinking Offers Comparative Advantage

ABSTRACT

The present paper highlights a set of variables to effect an improvement in higher education sector which currently is suffering from certain ailments. These variables are of software nature and well within the control of a teacher. These variables are duly supported by evidences gathered from the teachers at operational level. The study has set some objectives and also a methodology. The study finally arrives at certain conclusions.

Introduction

The higher education system in yester years churned out outstanding scholars, reputed scientists, acclaimed social thinkers, expert engineers, specialised physicians, eminent political leaders and above all well disciplined citizens. But now tertiary institutions are reduced to coaching shops for various examinations. However, entire scenario will change when the role of teacher is elevated to that of a scholar who engages himself in a continuous interaction with the students to stimulate learning while learning himself.

The Study

Rationale

The college education suffers from certain ailments. These ailments need remedial measures. The system could be reactivated and rejuvenated to serve the society at large. The hardware component may take some time as it relates to certain policy decisions outside the campus. However, software component of the campus operations could not wait for more time. The present study has been conducted in this backdrop with due focus on software component.

Objectives

The study aims at the following objectives:

1. To construct several performance measures in order to bring an efficiency in the institutional operations.
2. To gather the response of a select group of college teachers to the performance measures constructed as these do not require long-term policy frame work.
3. To motivate educational stakeholders to continue with the debate and discussion to improve upon the academic productivity.

Methodology

The 14 dimensions constructed have been divided into two parts comprising 7 in each part. The verbal discussions held and an interview schedule was administered on a select group of 65 teachers functioning in different colleges in order to gather their valued opinion. However, 50 teachers responded well as desired and the response rate has been around 77 per cent. The qualitative performance measures thus constructed have been quantified by conversion with due support of likert scale (5-1). In order to draw certain inferences the statistical techniques like total weighted score, mean score, standard deviation, co-efficient of variance, mean score and rank in percentage have been computed. The said analysis of data is presented in tabular form to facilitate interpretation.

Results and Discussion

Following few areas summarised in two sections are to be considered with some passion.

Part-I: Integrated Approach

The academic performance needs strategic thinking in an era of comparative bench-marking. The institutions in government sector can also beat bench-marks when they work smart. Exemplary work culture and integrated approach thus adopted lead to excellence.

Thought process

The Higher Education Institutions (HEIs) are ideas and thought process organizations. These institutions are not confined to the transaction of regular course content alone but are actively engaged in research and extension activities as well. The faculty is required to be highly enthusiastic to contribute to the knowledge advancement.

Relevant pedagogy

The regular and effective delivery of course content no doubt is paramount. For improvement in the transaction, student-centric pedagogy should gain currency. The students are actively to be engaged in the process to think critically and analytically. Course content is to be analysed in such a fashion that different components in each unit are taken care of besides teacher-centered methodology through virtual classroom (Edu-Sat) and student conferencing.

Academic schedule

The weekly academic schedules (lesson plans) need be prepared accordingly and communicated to students in advance. The requisite infrastructure and expertise are developed in this regard. Research activities offer an advantage to be fully abreast with the current trends. Further, equal focus on event management, student laurels and faculty achievements is to be duly placed. Sincere efforts put in thus will effect a positive change in the system.

Scientific temper

The colleges desire to be excellent academic institutions to promote love for lifelong learning. Graduate programme is a three-year long grind to inculcate scientific temper. Motivating students to participate in diverse activities on the campus need to develop a sense of disciplined life. Campus life will be rich when open dialogue is appreciated, spirit of inquiry is encouraged and analytical orientation is promoted.

Skill development

The best way to acquire appropriate skills is learning-by-doing. The students accordingly need to be engaged for soft skills in institution building activities: organizing debates and guest sessions; managing events and maintaining discipline; arranging placements and career counseling. They shall be active participants in the learning process to get a feel of leadership. Interactive pedagogy shall be instructional strategy to affect excellence in classroom transactions. It shall result in multi-dimensional exchange of ideas and brainstorming on critical social and scientific issues. The evaluation thus needs a switchover from sheer memorisation capabilities to problem-solving and effective communication competencies.

Stakeholder dialogue

The stakeholder dialogue has a great significance in the academic performance of institutions of higher learning. Appraisal at 360 degree level is quite essential. Student feedback, Parent view point, faculty assessment and administrative response have added significance. Inclusiveness and carving space for all should be a step towards improvement in academic productivity.

Part-II: Creative Ideas

The process of developing a novel idea or a new way of approaching an old idea is creativity. In a competitive environment transformation of creative ideas through higher education process fulfills student needs. Following a routine and beaten track is to be replaced by the unique way of performance. Achievements shall not make complacent but performance deficit must render one uncomfortable and feel concerned.

Academic worth

The theoretical performance level needs to be deflated to the real intrinsic academic worth attained. Immediate attention

Table 12.1:

(N=50)

Dimensions	TWS	Mean Score	Std. Deviation	Co-officient of Variance	Rank	
					Mean in %	Status
Integrated Approach	207	4.14	0.321	7.753	82.80	R5
Thought Process	212	4.24	0.872	20.566	84.80	R1
Relevant Pedagor	211	4.22	0.754	17.867	84.40	R2
Academic Schedule	206	4.12	0.073	1.771	82.40	R6
Scientific Temper	209	4.18	0.997	23.852	83.60	R4
Skill Development	210	4.20	0.315	7.500	84.00	R3
Stakeholder Dialogue	205	4.10	0.203	4.951	82.00	R7

Source: The Table 12.1 highlights that different dimensions attracted the attention of sample respondents by assigning priorities. Thought process culminated with the highest priority whereas stakeholders dialogue ended up at the last The mean score in percentages ranged between 82 per cent and 84 per cent with standard deviation less than 1 reflecting stability across different dimensions. All the dimensions have been considered significant as regards improvement in higher education sector in the state.

is required with regard to teaching-learning-evaluation process enrichment towards creativity enabling learners to exhibit their hidden potential. Creativity ultimately sparks innovation. The colleges shall strive smart in pursuance of institutional vision and mission towards this end.

Spiritual laboratory

The concept of spiritual laboratory in the colleges will have far reaching implications with due regard to overall personality development of students. They are exposed to the hard realities of life to imbibe in them certain values to realise inner core of the person. If the system sans spiritual aspect of life a distinction between good and bad, right and wrong, true and false etc., cannot be made. There will be ethical deficit and total disorder and disconnect in the society. To ensure fair wheel to play in the society spiritual laboratory has an effective role to perform attune with inner being.

Innovative practices

The practice of transparency and disclosure results in seriousness and meticulous work behaviour. Competition offers more opportunities than threats. Education deficits push a society in isolation and in globalised world can prove more detrimental for socio-economic advancement. Creativity is the key to make departure from the routine way of learning. But we are still in qualifying the examination mode which requires a shift at the earliest.

Possibility thinking

The tendency to think and react negatively has no place in academics. Same is true with pessimism. Attitudinal change through possibility thinking coupled with strategic advantage needs to be made. Participation and team work boost emotional quotient. Updated dissemination with due support of latest research findings will enrich intellectual capital of the institutions and intrinsic academic worth of students in turn.

Academic documentation

The academic documentation has gained an added significance to showcase different activities organized by colleges during a particular period. The role played by the faculty in this context is required to be highly appreciated. The initiatives taken by the team of compilers in Colleges for starting the publication of periodic IQAC Newsletters and Quarterly Quantum (Higher Education Department) shall duly be acknowledged.

Institutional accreditation

The faculty and the staff need to look into the vital and critical issue of assessment and accreditation by according it topmost priority. The objective is to reinforce all stakeholders for their valued contribution towards academic advancement at individual level which will also serve as a competitive benchmark for the institutional excellence, also a pre-requisite for NAAC re-accreditation. Accreditation, being a continuous process, is reduced to a one time affair in five year period which needs to be changed.

Table 12.2

(N=50)

Dimensions	TWS	Mean Score	Std. Deviation	Co-officient of Variance	Rank	
					Mean in %	Status
Spiritual Lab.	210	4.20	0.897	21.357	84.00	R3
Academic Worth	215	4.22	0.314	7.441	84.40	R2
Possibility Thinking	207	4.14	0.606	14.637	82.80	R5
Acad. Documentation	204	4.11	0.980	23.844	82.20	R6
Institution Accreditation	205	4.10	0.521	12.707	82.00	R7
Innovative Practices	208	4.16	0.499	11.995	83.20	R4
Creative Ideas	214	4.24	0.697	16.438	84.80	R1

Source: The Table 12.2 in the same fashion focused on creative ideas and terminated at institutional accreditation by attracting R1 and R7 respectively. The mean score in percentage also was registered more than 80 per cent in between 82.00 per cent and 84.80 per cent the different dimensions also reflected stability as the standard deviation ranged from 0.314 and 0.980.

Conclusion

The bottom-line arrived at in the context of aforesaid discussion is passion for superb performance. The students accordingly need be motivated to plan their own time to shape their career with a view to come up on top. The need of the hour demands a change through intellectual strengths and capabilities in the entire education system. In sum, college faculty has to play a role of cheerleaders, facilitators and mentors to be differentiated under new paradigm.

REFERENCES

Yash Pal (2012), "An Optimistic Future for Indian Education", *Yojna,* 56:5-7.

Dubashi, PR (2012), "Educational Reforms in Finland", *South Asia Politics,* 11(4): 15-16.

VilanilamJ V (2012), "Development of Education in India 1947-2012, *Yojna,* 56: 28-33.

Gilkar, N A (2012), "Dignity of Labour is Paramount", *Rising Kashmir,* 6 (233):7.

APPENDIX – I

RE-ENGINEERING UG CURRICULUMS: FOCUS ON DEVELOPMENT OF HARD SKILLS

The UGC vocational scheme launched in 1994 failed because of ineffective academic-industry interface. Similarly, UGC add-on-courses programme started in 2004 has not taken off simply owing to its non-mandatory nature. A degree certificate is awarded purely on the memorisation of course content with no regard to real learning and skill (hard as well as soft) development. Very recently UNESCO came out with certain recommendations for improving education sector so as:

- To make academics more practical-oriented.
- To affect changes in curriculum and innovations in the methods of teaching.
- To organize special classes for teachers for effective and powerful delivery.
- To launch Honors with a view to enable students demonstrate proficiency.
- To introduce Continuous Comprehensive Evaluation (CCE) system.
- To put evaluation system in place through teacher-student accountability.

The Honours programmes in the disciplines like English and Commerce have already been launched from the current academic session (2012) despite stiff resistance by the affiliating university. More and More Honrs programmes to cover all subjects to be introduced at the earliest the better. The Honrs programmes are offered purely based on merit to forge a vertical academic and research integration. The students are required to put in more intellectual rigour as the course content is designed in a high caliber fashion. The class attendance of students in such courses understandably is encouraging and they are very serious in pursuit of knowledge and accordingly work smart.

The general or pass degree courses conversely should be open for all. The course structure of pass degree courses in the first instance needs re-engineering to be reduced from 4 to 3 courses of study for imparting scholastic content. The 4th one shall be a mandatory hardware course with due reference to dignity of labour in order to develop hard skills in one or the other vocation/trade. The dignity of labour during the current times demands to be paramount.

The UGC-academic staff colleges need to organize teaching pedagogy workshops for teachers to focus on student-centric instructional strategies. The participants shall deliberate upon innovative teaching strategies and analyse those in practice over the period with due academic efficacy thereof. The sole objective is to provoke students to think. This shall lead to solve a problem in real life situation. The book based learning need necessarily be subordinate to real life learning. Student-centric methodology has to be given a due space enabling students to learn the concepts well rather than memorise the text material.

The Government has not to create jobs only but to provide an environment for job and wealth creation. The very three important organs like affiliating university, EDI, and Department of labour and employment need to operate in tandem to find out ways and means leading to entrepreneurship as well as skill development in basic trades/vocations as are in demand in the local job market. The students during their stay on the campus shall necessarily have to be engaged in such activities enabling them to learn soft skills besides their intellectual development.

The national vocational education qualification framework (NVEQF) envisaged for Jammu and Kashmir has not kick started as yet. The scheme even if launched will not yield the desired results because it being optional for the students. However, for acquiring hard skills the students are to be referred to industry and other relevant institutes during winter vacations. This shall be a mandatory and result-oriented component of the curriculum.

The entire examination business shall accordingly be completed by the end of December. A shift from closed-end to open-ended book examination is desired to be made. It is generally observed that effective teacher-taught interaction in colleges is for a limited period spread over certain months only resulting in a disconnect. However, the aforesaid proposal will help in maintaining on and off campus good connect.

The introduction of single paper scheme for term end examination makes CCE essential. It could serve twin objectives-relief from stress and reduction in examination cycle. There will be a good blending between learning and evaluation. The students will always be prepared for continuous evaluation. However, equal weightage is to be accorded to both-internal evaluation and external examination.

The institutions shall organize sensitisation programmes to motivate students to affect a change in their mindset with a view to prepare themselves for selecting a particular vocation/ trade to be trained in to earn livelihood in a dignified way immediately after being qualified graduates. This way Gross Enrolment Ratio (GER) can further be improved upon and a solution for unemployment also sought out. The status of simple/pass BA/B. Sc/B. Com duly blended with hard skills would be a terminal programme as more and more Honours programmes are being launched. The preset triple objective of attitude-knowledge-skill can thus be easily achieved.

APPENDIX – II

REINVENT ACADEMIC LEADERSHIP: THE PROFESSIONAL ETHICS AUDIT

Preface

The SMART academic governance has the features like systematic, motivated, accountable, responsive, transparent governance. The world is moving fast toward outcomes. The work experience is made more enjoyable when one is proactive. Be proactive is one of the seven habits of highly effective people (covey). Innovations, diversifications and fair play add credibility to the whole process of governance.

We need to 'sharpen the saw' and adopt a set of virtues that could help in bringing efficacy in the governance and the system at large. Do improve upon knowledge-values-skills (wisdom-virtues-competencies) to render the best possible actions. Honesty, truthfulness, courage, punctuality, contentment are the most important leadership qualities. Staying smart to give a 'feel change' is deliberated upon in this context.

Do Question

The essence of a question stands realised. When we say 'what', we ask because we want to know. But, when we say 'How' and 'Why' we question. We question the very premise – the paradigm. We want a change in the status-quo and combat stereo – break inertia and revolutionise life.

To question-needs a considerable intellectual understanding and higher order of emotional depth. It requires intellectual courage par excellence. An intelligent question may not have an instant intelligent answer. It is a process and it continues. Miles are to go before we arrive at the truth.

Question was raised by Hussain (RA) in the field of Karbala in the 6th century and Copernicus in the 16th century. Observance of ethical obligations and lawful duties with sincerity, zeal and devotion utilising the best of one's capacity is essential.

Leader is a change agent as he advocates but practices as well a shift from one paradigm to another. Focus is on unlearning some old work habits and relearning. One has to be ready for supreme sacrifice as well, while raising a question.

Mahatma Gandhi Mohandas Karamchand desired to adopt governance model practiced by Umer-II Caliph for independent India. He otherwise had a governance model available in the Arthshastra by Kautaliya or well known as Chankiya. However Qaid-i-Azam Mohammad Ali Jinnah well known for his wit and wisdom did not adopt such a model of governance for newly created state based on two nations theory. What a paradox it is? Needs a response.

Be Wise

The wisdom teaches us how to deliver results in uncertain times. Leadership is inborn to a degree, but it can be acquired through effort. Leaders of all times must possess ability to lead change.

In times of change thinking as usual does not work. The old mental models based on history and experience no longer hold good. In the evolving life of a human society conflict is inevitable.

Accordingly events are conducted to study and analyse the phenomenon in pursuance of preset vision, mission, goals and objectives. In this context efforts are being made to achieve the desired outcome with due regard to synergy *i.e.* (2+2=4 effect).

Outcome-effort relationship guides that any of the situation may take place: gain, break-even or loss. It is essential to measure this relationship in tangible terms focusing on quantification of results and effort. Structural and behavioural experts developed befitting models based on variety of statements on both the dimensions by applying relevant techniques.

Observe Honesty

The old saying is 'honesty is the best policy'. Honesty under its umbrella covers a wide range of issues. To what extent one performs that evaluates honesty in one's field of work. It is not confined to financial matters alone.

An honest person is law abiding and does not lie. We want to be decent in giving an honest answer, an honest appraisal of ability can only help. One has to be honest while dealing with other stakeholders operating in the system. In teaching-learning-evaluation process it is academic honesty.

Honest work is job done fairly well. Honest living is money earned by working hard and smart as required. Similarly, honest truth is the complete truth-to be above all small minded prejudices. Honesty and truth are similar to straight lines that go parallel. Conversely, dishonesty and lying are just twisted and sloping lines. An honest mistake is unintentional.

"It was a known fact that the suppliers had a margin for me and the office. We generally entered into a negotiation even after the process of tendering was complete. Sequel to which they were paid less than the bill amount in order to give them a realisation that we work in the best interest of the organization. This act was appreciated".

Value Time

The behavioural experts opine that punctuality is the first sign of loyalty towards an organization. Punctuality refers to starting as well as completing work at right time. Punctuality guides in 'Put first-things-first' as well as 'begin with ends in mind'.

Usually there are habitual late comers in every organization. Being late is a shameful situation not approved of. The Englishmen put on wrist-watch to exercise punctuality. Conversely, we put it on simply as an ornament for show. Perhaps our culture in general has written off the habit of being on time.

The work-culture is an important determinant not just for the economic growth and advancement but equally for the quality of social life. There is a saying 'time and tide wait for none'. The careless approach to maintain proper timing results in wastage of an invaluable resource as wastage of time means wastage of money. Being consistently late, one strains relationship with fellow workers and colleagues.

The focus on punctuality is the fore runner to improve upon work efficacy. The value of ill-effects associated with non-punctuality need an in-depth study. Steps are to be initiated to compute the impact of non-punctuality on performance and productivity.

The value added employment of people has a special characteristic of being punctual. It needs realisation and self-motivation. By giving up 'tomorrow culture' we prove productive. Punctuality will revolutionize the socio-economic inertia the society is confronted with. Work ethics and work etiquettes are essential requisites in every culture.

Punctuality reflects respect and consideration for fellow-feeling and organizational commitment. Punctuality is not simply a time skill. But a relationship quality and a manifestation of personal character as well. The habit of punctuality is amazing as it exhibits how life becomes organized with time.

The societies move forward through investment in human capital underpinned by a variety of values including punctuality. Objectivity demands leaders adhere firmly to the principles of equity and justice leading to transformation of social fabric.

Exhibit Courage

The importance of courage can hardly be overstated. Courage is the capability to perform right or good, despite doing it is difficult or dangerous. Courageous people always think win-win. 'They create a level field for every player'. 'They do not do to others what they do not wish others do to them.

To dissent a corrupt, violent or wrong doer is a reflection of immense courage. Really, it is courageous to admit a mistake or a wrong doing. 'Every saint has a past and every sinner a future'. Try to feel brave enough to do something non-routine and against the tide. Do not encourage wrong doers; rather, curtail their injurious actions.

A great deal of courage needs to avoid a friend if found wrong. Courage is the competence to face in calm terrible and acute pain. Hence, courage is exhibited in one's own conviction to perpetuate doing the right even when people think otherwise.

The courageous and assertive are more confident, optimistic and hopeful because of fair work conduct. To decide to perform even though one being frightened about it is an achievement.

It needs to go beyond wishful to willful act. 'The first inhibits action and the second inspires action'. Wishful is a passing fancy or a weak impulse in the mind that does not translate into action. Willful makes more decisive that one decides to act. A courageous is very brave, balanced and determined in his commitment. Courage and honesty run parallel.

A leader must never, as Richard Nixon says in his book LEADERS, 'suffer paralysis through analysis'. Napoleon said that two-thirds of decision-making is based on study, analysis, calculations, facts and figures, but the other third is always a leap in the dark, based on one's gut. Anyone who increases that one-third is too impulsive (Musharaf: 2006).

Be good to yourself-this implies nurturing and improving positive energies and impulses, and disciplining negative ones. This tale of courage and sacrifice has power to ignite more such efforts like a lamp lighting other lamps.

Decision Power

The wining starts with beginning and beginning starts with a single action. Today's decisions are tomorrow's realities. To really be successful in life, all it is to be done: *(i)* get started, and *(ii)* never quit.

"Winisten Churchil prime minister of the UK during World War-II was invited to deliver key-note address. There was pin drop silence. And he spoke thus: never-never-never-

never give up. Having spoken these five words only in his address there was a total hush. However, this great message soon sank home and he received a long standing ovation".

Academic leaders govern the institutions of higher education from the front. They accept challenges and do not believe in escapism. So they are different. My age guides me to boost their morale.

Handle ideas by making a decision. People in the organizations respond to new ideas in different ways. Hibernates run away because they may have to put in more effort. Luxuriate do not pay much attention to new ideas as they are easy going. Commiserate argue it is tried so often. Procrastinates put off acting and are not ready yet.

No doubt a leader has to be caring .But, remember that equilibrium must not be disturbed. Caring and abiding shall move parallel. An effective leader has always been a 'force multiplier'.

In such a situation pick up positive, but not negative attitudes. Be positive – it inspires positive emotions and provokes positive results – confidence, optimism, contentment, courage. Whereas negative thinking stimulates negative emotions and promotes negative results-worry, distress, sadness suspicion (Schuller: 1988).

Self-discipline

The Ineffectiveness in operations stems when people in the organization do not exhibit self-discipline. They do not perform in accordance with the knowledge and training they have been developed. Sequel to which there is negative Performance Gap. Leader is a liberator and not a limiter of people's highest talents as he leads by heart. Vision, dreams, idealism and a skill set in terms of communication etc., relate to managing by mind.

Leadership is not about managing things but about developing people; producing leaders and not followers. The leaders groom sub-leaders and smoothen the way for succession planning. In an educational organization a variety of sub-leaders under the leadership at the apex level lead different operational segments. Thus the number of leaders churned out by a leader is to be evaluated.

Once paycheck online sans linkage to sincerity of purpose by the led in the organization he is engaged in micro management. The shift from negative to positive performance gap could be ensured only when: *(i)* professional ethics audit, and *(ii)* performance budgeting are pressed in practice.

Have Initiative

The one with initiative makes a happening. A man with initiative is self-starter that makes him dynamic. An effective leader is always two jumps ahead of events. Possibility Thinking is his eternal belief.

Learning is a life-long and perpetual endeavour knowledge is power. Job and environment knowledge offer a leader strength. The reading habit is the biggest single factor contributing toward indirect experience. An inquisitive open-mind and acceptance of informed criticism are essential requirements for enrichment and growth of a leader. He strives tirelessly to meet the academic performance targets set by the organization in consonance with the global bench-marks.

Communication and understanding human nature inter alia constitute a skill set that help to perform as effective leader. An effective leader knows his people quite well. In an organization people do have either vested interest behaviour or rule based behaviour. The former look at individual welfare alone. Whereas, the latter have a due regard for societal interest.

Shun Self

The objective was to knock my conscience. Come what may one has to face the truth one day. The material gains do not last long. Why then one works day in and day out in pursuit of material welfare?

The tangible happiness one finds in contentment. Whatsoever is available, enjoy to the fullest. Contentment – what in possession-does not make a person look beyond? Self-centered people are never satisfied. Enjoy life-prefer to be selfless than selfish-shun the greed. 'Where need ends greed begins'.

The truth focus on actual facts about a phenomenon. Rather, than what people think or expect. The fact of the matter is that the truth may never be known. Most people are doubtful about the truth what one says.

Universal or eternal truth is that courageous do not care to tell the truth. People will find out the truth about something even if it is tried to keep it a secret. Truthful person says what is true and never tells a lie. A truthful book deals with a subject in an honest way by sharing what really happens in a particular situation. Thus be truthful, avoiding injury and harm to innocent.

Epilogue

Thus, a leader:

1. Unlearns some old work habits with the passage of time and relearns many new ones to proceed ahead in his career.
2. Leads a change to achieve the target outcome by putting in effort with a blending of pro-active approach and synergy.
3. Maintains equilibrium between caring and abiding as he is a 'force multiplier'.
4. Exhibits courage and is assertive and creates a win-win situation for all stakeholders.
5. Ensures punctuality and disapproves 'Tomorrow Culture'.
6. Produces leaders, not followers and guides in succession planning.
7. Takes initiative proves self-starter and dynamic.
8. Strives tirelessly to meet academic performance targets set by the organization.
9. Prioritises societal interest to his individual interest.
10. Self-less in word and deed and finds tangible happiness in contentment.

APPENDIX – III

DEVIL'S ADVOCACY

BUSINESS EDUCATION IN KASHMIR: RETHINKING STRATEGIES IN K-SOCIETY PERSPECTIVE BUT BEFORE THAT

The present write up prefers rationalism over perceptual or empirical foundations of acquiring knowledge. Reasoning-rational or logical-is the basis of gaining such knowledge. Rational knowledge is the higher level compared to other two. Ideas formation is the construction material for critical and analytical thinking. The methods that assist a learner/researcher to gather answers contribute towards enrichment of mind. Rationalists therefore propound that the method of pure reason is the most accurate way of gaining knowledge. Mind has the capability to discover truth. Wisdom suggests comparing ideas with ideas. Devil's Advocacy asks to know. A dialogue is arranged with a view to make a true assessment of the state of affairs in this context.

Part – I

The business education constitutes all the programmes covered under commerce and management delivered at college as well as university level. The programmes like B. com; BBA; M. com; MFC; MBA; M. Phil; PhD; DLitt fall under the domain of business education offered by the higher education institutions operating both in public and private sectors in Kashmir as well. The civil society asks to know and find answers before rethinking strategies to uplift the business education standards in Kashmir in knowledge society (k-society) perspective.

The principal, Sri Ram College of Commerce, New Delhi Dr. SP Jain says that: *(a)* he established a college of commerce in Assam at the advice of Prime Minister of India Dr. Man Mohan Singh; *(b)* his two colleagues are earning Rs. one crore each in terms of consultancy services offered a year; *(c)* his three colleagues are earning Rs. fifty lakh each in terms of royalty on the books published a year. Where do we stand in the aforesaid scenario?

A top bureaucrat in the civil secretariat who incidentally was my class fellow during a colloquium asked. Are you engaged in tuition practice? I did not reply in affirmative. 'Then you must have written books and earned royalty'. Private tutoring is not approved of because not producing more than forty professionals in sixty six years against three hundred did our counter parts the other side of the Jawahar Tunnel. There should have been a queue of chartered accountants/ cost and management accountants/chartered secretaries/ financial analysts keeping in view the size of private tutoring centres in accounting discipline.

The professional business academics are busy in writing books, research papers, monographs, general articles, book reviews etc. These are published in journals of repute with a high impact factor and wide citation at national and international levels. How many academic papers written by the faculty (including me) associated with Business Education have been published year-wise in Harvard Business Review?

We have not developed content editing and language editing R and D Labs by professional editors in business education research. It is not possible to attain excellence in research in absence of such an academic culture.

The business academics have not engaged themselves in thought process to add to the existing fund of knowledge. They simply have compiled that sans original contribution. Primarily being bereft of research methodology, creative ideas and theorizing of concepts are the main responsible factors. Economics has a wide canvas where as commerce and management has shrunk the space. It may be because of its skill orientation focus against thought process.

The course content is transacted through a variety of application oriented instructional strategies that include case studies as well enabling students to doubt, ask and question. How many case studies, occasional papers, status write ups, guidance notes are prepared by the faculty for open discussion a year?

The business education has its own form and content. Accordingly, the strategic intent is to create student value addition in its unique style. How many teaching pedagogies with special reference to and relevance of business education in k-society have been developed and put in practice during last three years by the faculty?

The professional business academics are always busy in reviewing, revising, designing and developing new courses of study and programmes relevant to contemporary times. How many new and different courses of study designed and developed by the faculty have got academic concurrence?

The affiliating university is not ready to design and develop BFC programme whereas MFc programme is now in operation for last one decade. A new programme which may be introduced at a right time after meeting all procedural requirements by the concerned stakeholders. But first design and develop some new programmes.

The professors in recognition of their contribution generally are invited by the Government as advisors in different areas of governance or appointed as commission chairmen or members. Has any business academic so far been invited by the Government to perform as advisor?

The true business education is a blending of academic activity and application in industry and services sector. Business academics generally invest some time in industry to understand the real problems and find their solutions. How many faculty members have corporate exposure in terms of years they have put in?

The institutions of higher learning like colleges and universities are now strategic and known by their vision and mission generally highlighted in all the institutional published documents. How many faculty members remember the vision, mission, goals and objectives of their respective institutions and direct their activities toward their realisation?

The outcome-effort correlation is essential as regards academic growth, dynamism and institutional productivity. Of course in pure academics outcome justifies effort. Has the focus of the faculty been toward outcome or simply on effort with no correlation with outcome?

The faculty must be highly enthusiastic and self-motivated to be well recognised in the society for scholarship and not only by the creation of estate as done by ordinary people who are interested in online salary cheque at the month end. No people are above the level of its teachers. No space for pseduoism or short cuts is recommended. Teachers alone are change agents in the society. Have the business academics appetite for satisfying self-actualisation need?

The faculty is generally associated with academic professional bodies. They are periodically consulted and their valued opinion sought on vital issues. How many faculty members are associated with national level professional bodies for periodic consultations?

The instruction in business education generally is text book oriented. It is simply dissemination of information. Select numerical or text material with due focus on examination constitutes the entire gamut of the business education. No focus on knowledge or wisdom or life. No focus on inculcation of virtues or ethics or skill development. Sequel to it the pass outs prefer class 4th or low profile drudgery jobs available in the market. Sheer wastage of men and money........... Am I not answerable for this mess before my society?

Part – II

The primary objective of higher education is to produce leaders for different segments of society. Higher education institutions are required to play their designated role. Debate, discussion and dialogue are the beauty of higher learning institutions. And for this structural capital though modest is created. Civil society is interested in uplift of social standards.

The future of the society is shaped in the class room. Have class rooms been converted into centres of intellectual capital or knowledge centres and institutions of higher learning into human development campuses?

The advent of third generation technology accelerated class-room transaction and improved productivity of outcome. How many class rooms are state-of-the-art fitted with all the necessary gadgets in each institution?

No doubt such facilities are created in the institutions. There can be a cluster of colleges in every district to share mutually the physical and faculty resources. The students from colleges established in the recent past shall be sent to the established institutions to attend some sessions conducted by the senior faculty. They will also get an opportunity to interact with the faculty and students there. Yes, faculty resources need rationalisation at the earliest to avoid institution-wise mismatch.

The educational process is the multiple function of=f (k, v, s). Has there been a specific session for spiritual laboratory, R and D laboratory, Dialogue and Defense in the weekly schedule?

The virtues can either be imbibed by practice or even taught by narration. Two instances can easily be quoted here:

"One day, while Chankiya was doing his office work at night, a friend of his walked in to have a chat with him. Chankiya immediately put out one oil lamp and lighted another. The friend was astonished and Chankiya explained him that the oil in the first lamp was provided by the king and that oil in the second was purchased by him. The first lamp was only to be used for office work. This was the commitment to ethical values".

A young boy brought into his home a small branch of a poplar tree from the compound of the mosque in the vicinity. On seeing the same his parents and grandmother were shivered and turned pale. The grandmother rushed to the kitchen and got a piece of chopped wood used as fuel for mud stoves those days. She threw the same into the compound of the mosque to compensate. This way the boy was taught a lifelong lesson.

The real learning takes place when more space is created for the learners enabling them to develop an inquisitive mind.

A continuous thirst for knowledge is created but never quenched. A learner must always be demanding. Teacher alone can create such an academic environment on the campus. Has student centric-learning been accorded a dominant role?

The educational technology has facilitated teaching-learning process as in the global village space is shrunk that enabled the faculty across world to enjoy a quite easy access. Has some specific content in each course of study been identified for transaction through Edu-sat?

The time table is to be framed in such a way to avoid any kind of overlapping between traditional and virtual class-room.

The role of a teacher in the k-society has changed. He is now a facilitator, a mentor, a coach. The syllabus is analysed into small segments unit-wise enabling students to search for required material and forget those manufactured study notes available at a price in the bazar that crippled the critical, analytical and inquisitive mental faculties of learners. Do the students stand informed fortnights in advance with regard to the Day-wise transaction of course content relevant to different subjects?

Not good it is in the academic interests that disconnect persists between scholarship and corporate practice. Scholarship has an edge over practice. Vice versa is not true. Creative and innovative ideas are generated in educational institutions and practiced at the work place. What is the role of practitioners, professionals, alumni from the industry and profession respectively in strategic value addition of students?

The essence of learning is to develop an ability to ask and question. It is possible only when students always keep their mind active in possibility thinking. They are motivated to study varied books besides prescribed syllabi. Have students been offered an opportunity to be actively engaged in thought process by questioning the very premise or paradigm?

The institutions of higher learning offer space for dissent. There can be either vested interest behaviour or rule based behaviour. Optimism, positive mindset and possibility thinking is the reflection of latter but not the former behaviour.

Teaching is assessed and learning evaluated. Teaching must result in learning. It is not a simple process. But teachers are not ready for their assessment by their students. Has teaching-learning-evaluation been considered a cyclical process with due interdependence on each other?

The present era focuses on micro-specialisations in every branch of knowledge. We generally quote Kotler, Drucker, Porter or even Ponday and Shukla because they have made adequate real contribution in the literature available on business education programmes. Have our professional business academics made any remarkable and original contribution well recognised at global level?

The canvas of aforesaid dialogue can be enlarged by the faculty and students pursuing their studies in the colleges and universities provided it is taken in the right perspective. Structural facilities whatsoever created in our institutions need optimal utilisation for collective gain.

Part – III

The losses suffered in real academics can mostly be attributed to examinations and evaluation. It is a British colonial legacy that examinations dominated the entire education system. Student focus contrary to real learning is on passing examinations. This attitude toward examinations and evaluation needs a change earlier the best.

The marks card is single dimensional evaluation sheet ignoring other aspects of life. Institution develops integrated personality of students. While on campus a student is exposed to a variety of challenges that offer him varied opportunities in real life. Has marks card been replaced by score card detailing the participation of students in all activities carried on the campus?

The business education primarily focuses on skill development. It has adopted a different style of teaching. So is required of examinations and evaluation as well. Examinations need not be only student friendly but civil society has a stake as well. How business education examination pattern is different from other disciplines-sciences, social sciences and Humanities?

The components of curriculum management are open-ended and impact each other. Has evaluation resulted into enhancement of learning and personality development of students or otherwise?

The contemporary times demand open-ended as against closed-end approach with regard to examinations preferably in business education. Have examination techniques like open-book, no-supervision, self-evaluation etc., been put in practice?

The post LPG era is open, transparent and nothing is concealed so is true with examinations and evaluation. Has focus of evaluation been on disclosure by highlighting question-wise marks awarded?

The post examination and evaluation period is very crucial and guides to design strategies for further improvement. Have after thorough analyses of answer scripts reasons ascertained as to why students attempted particular questions generally and left some other questions unattended to at all?

The core objective is to affect efficacy by chiseling the hidden talent of students. Has teaching-learning-evaluation process been able to develop value added human resource with due honing of talent to lead effectively different segments of society with special focus on corporate governance?

The confidence level thus attained will indicate the capability to face the challenges of real life. Effective education system produces leaders to lead from the front. Have students been able to solve real life problems confronting the society?

The application of educational technology has improved productivity of teaching-learning-evaluation process. Has technology been used as support service or students made subservient to such services?

The perpetual student monitoring and performance audit is utility oriented preferably in the post NAAC period. Has student performance during their stay on the campus been regularly judged based on 4Cs: *(i)* confidence; *(ii)* communication; *(iii)* content; *(iv)* competence?

The focus is on content dissemination in the class room situation. This encourages rote memorisation. No effort is made with regard to contextual analysis. Has there been a shift from evaluating know-how to know-why?

The real capital of a student is his mind set than the learning of functional skills. A student should seriously gear up not merely for a depository of accumulation of facts but realisation of social aspirations. Does change in student mind set form a component in evaluation process?

The aforesaid debate and discussion suggests that immediate need is to rethink and redesign strategies to revamp examination system so that the business education in Kashmir meets the emerging demands of K-society. The student strategic value creation is primarily related to faculty performance though other stakeholders have also a positive role.

Bibliography

A. Gani (1995), "Workshop on Re-orientation of Commerce Curriculum – A Report", *The Business Review*, 1(1); 103 to 105.

Agarwal V. and Bhatnagar R. P. (2004), Educational Administration: Supervision, Planning and Financing, Surva Publishing, Meerut.

Agarwal, A. G. (1994), "Role of Management Accountant in Liberalised Economy". *The Management Accountant*, 29(9): 650-652.

Agarwal, G. C. (1992), "Excellence in Business Education", Prof. A. Das Memorial Lecture, SLV All India Commerce Conference, University of Bangalore.

Agarwal, J. C. (1960), Teaching of Commerce: A Practical Approach, Vikas Publishing House Pvt. Ltd., New Delhi.

Alvin Toffler (1991), "Future Sheeks".

Azam, M. K. (1999), "Proactive Approach to Accounting Education", *The Management Accountant*, 34(5): 371-372.

Bhatcharya, *et al.,* (1984), "Accounting for Managers", Vani Educational Books, New Delhi.

Bhatia and Bhatia (1994), The Principles and Methods of Teaching, Doba House Publishers, Delhi.

Bloom, B. S. (1956), Taxonomy of Educational Objectives, Handbook I Cognitive Domain, McKay.

Cenger JA and Kanungo RN (1998), The Empowerment Process: Integrating Theory and Practice, *Academy of Management Journal*, 13, 471-482.

Chakraborly. R. K. (2006), "Cost Control to Result Control – The New Business Challenge for the 21st' Century", *The Chartered Accountant*. 55(03). 427-432.

Dubashi, PR (2012), "Educational Reforms in Finland", *South Asia Politics*, 11(4): 15-16.

Fayyaz Ahmad, Sayyed (1998), Vocationsation of Business Education in India: Implementation, Constraints and Opportunities, *The Business Review*, 4(1 and 2): 11-20.

Garg. VP (2006), "Budget Formulation for Educational Planning, Economic *vs.* Financial Approach", *NIEPA Bulletin NIEPA*, 7(1 and 2),42.

Gilkar, N A (2012), "Dignity of Labour is Paramount", Rising Kashmir: 6(233): 7.

Gilkar, N. A. (2004), "Streamlining the Examination System", Greater Kashmir, Dec. 10, p. 7.

Gilkar, Nazir Ahmad (2002), Commerce Education in Kashmir: A Study, Book Vision, Srinagar.

Gilkar. NA (2008), "Performance Budgeting m Higher Education Institutions", in Financial Sector of India (edit) by Dr. R. K. Uppal. New Century Publications, New Delhi 50-59.

Gupta, SK and Sharma, R. K. (2007), Management Accounting, Kalyani Publishers, New Delhi.

Hindu (2004), "Outsourcing will Enhance Job Prospects", News Item; Oct. 21: 18.

ICFA University (2006), Management Accounting.

Jain, SP, Narang KL, Dhingra, TR (2002), Cost Accounting: Principles and Practice, Kalyana Publishers, Ludhiana.

Jan Kounser (2011), Fast but False, G. K., 24, No 297, p. 9.

John Mercer (2004), "Performance Based Budgeting".

Mohan V. K. M. (2008), "Building a Resultocracy" The Business Line, August 1 1-12.

NAAC (2001), "Manual for Self-Study for Affiliated/ Constituent Colleges, National Assessment and Accreditation Council, Bangalore: 16 to 32. 1.

Nikam, R. S, (1999), "Some Emerging Issues in Accounting Education and Profession", *The Indian Journal of Commerce*, 54(4): 20.

Oswal, ML and Agarwal, RI (1982), "Performance Budgeting" *The Management Accountant*, 17(4) 203-206.

Pancrar, U. (2005), "Performance Budgeting for Government Operations".

Pathan, S. N. (2005), Quality Improvement Programme in Higher Education through NAAC, Intellectual Book Bureau, Bhopal.

Pathan, S. N (2005), Quality Improvement Programme in Higher Education through NAAC, Intellectual Book Bureau, Bhopal.

Pattnayak B (2001), Human Resource Management Prentice Hall of India, New Delhi.

Prasad, J. (1993), "Stress on Skills" Business, Business India, Sept. 13-16.

Rather, A. R. (2002), "Towards Multi Talent Teaching Approach", Insight, 1(8): 75-84.

Reddy, S. G. (2006), Industry Business Institute Interaction for Quality Management Education, University News.

Shankaran, Scncider and Douglas (1991), "Preparation of Accounting Graduates for Professional Accounting Career in the USA". *Chartered Accountant*, XXXX(9): 564-567.

Sharma, B.C. and Singh, W.C. (2007), "Re-defining Commerce Education in India", Arth Anvesan, 2(1): 31-34.

Sharma, S. L. (2004), "Higher Education and Quality Control: Some Reflections", See Higher Education in India: Problems and Prospects, 133-146.

Shukia, PD (1983), "Administration of Education in India", Vikas Publishing House Pvt. Ltd., New Delhi.

Sidiqui, M. A. (2004), "Teacher Development and Quality Education", See Mehraj-ud-Din (Ed.) Higher Education in India: Problems and Prospects, 107-118.

Tiwari, Arvind Kishore (2007), Industry – University/Business School Interaction for Quality Management/Commerce Education, in V. K. Singh (Edit), Innovations in Management Practices, Macmillan India Ltd.

UGC (1993), Vocationlisation of First Degree Education, New Delhi.

Vilanilam, V (2012), "Development of Education in India, 1947-2012, *Yojna*, 56: 28-33.

Wley A (l934), The Way and The Power: A Study of the Tao Te Ching and its Place in Chinese thought, Alleny and Lawlleo E. (1992). The Ultimate Advantage, Jossey-Bass, San Francisco, CA Greenberg J. and Barren R. (1997), Behaviour in Organization, 6th Edition, Prentice-Holen, Upper Saddle River, NJ.

Yash Pal (2012), "An Optimistic Future for Indian Education", *Yojna*, 56:5-7.

Index